YAKAMA RISING

Yakama Rising

Indigenous Cultural Revitalization, Activism, and Healing

MICHELLE M. JACOB

FIRST PEOPLES
New Directions in Indigenous Studies

THE UNIVERSITY OF
ARIZONA PRESS

TUCSON

All author royalties are being donated to the Northwest Indian Language Institute to support their ongoing work with tribal language teachers. By purchasing this book, you are directly contributing to indigenous language and culture revitalization efforts. Kw'ałanúushamash! (I am grateful to you!)

The University of Arizona Press
www.uapress.arizona.edu

Printed in the United States of America

Cover illustration: Silhouette from istock@seamartini
Cover design by Nicole Hayward

Publication of this book is made possible, in part, with a grant from the Andrew W. Mellon Foundation and by the proceeds of a permanent endowment created with the assistance of a Challenge Grant from the National Endowment for the Humanities, a federal agency.

Library of Congress Cataloging-in-Publication Data
Jacob, Michelle M., 1977–
    Yakama rising : indigenous cultural revitalization, activism, and healing / Michelle M. Jacob.
        p. cm.
    Includes bibliographical references and index.
    ISBN 978-0-8165-3049-6 (cloth : alk. paper)
    ISBN 978-0-8165-3119-6 (paperback : alk. paper)
    1. Yakama Indians—Social conditions.   2. Yakama Indians—Politics and government.
3. Yakama Indians—Ethnic identity.   4. Postcolonialism—Washington (State)—Yakama Indian Reservation.   5. Social change—Washington (State)—Yakama Indian Reservation.   6. Yakama Indian Reservation (Wash.)—History.   7. Yakama Indian Reservation (Wash.)—Race relations.   8. Yakama Indian Reservation (Wash.)—Politics and government.   I. Title.
    E99.Y2J33 2013
    305.897'41270797—dc23
                                                                                    2013009674

This book is dedicated to my favorite teachers, my parents.

Contents

Illustrations

Figures

Acknowledgments

Many people provided encouragement, insight, and assistance to make this book possible. I am inspired by my family, who never hesitate to be generous or thoughtful. Loving thanks to Dad, Mom, Uncle Jim, Roger, Gina, Garret, Hunter, Faith, Justin, Alicia, Quintic, Hazen, Blaise, and Sealy. I am blessed with in-laws who are exceptionally kind and considerate; thank you John, Karen, Dean, and Gloria. I am grateful to all the people who volunteered to be interviewed for this book. Your work to revitalize indigenous culture and language is an incredible gift. Thank you for sharing your stories. Research support was generously provided by University of San Diego (USD) Faculty Research Grants. Thank you to Dr. Alberto Pulido and Dean Mary Boyd for your leadership and vision to support community-based scholarship. Special thanks to my USD departmental colleagues: Gail Perez, Jesse Mills, and May Fu. Huge thanks to Esther Aguilar for your constant administrative support and kindness. Mary Jo Poole provided skillful transcription and many words of encouragement. Several people gave generous feedback on early drafts of chapters; thanks Tom Reifer, Judy Liu, Kathy Rolison, Jesse Mills, Gail Perez, Belinda Lum, LaShaune Johnson, Chris Andersen, and Theresa Jacob. Final manuscript revisions were made during my sabbatical, supported by USD. During my sabbatical, I had the honor of working with excellent and inspiring colleagues at Heritage University on the Yakama Reservation, where we launched the Center for Native Health & Culture. Thank you to the First Peoples: New Directions in Indigenous Studies Series and the University of Arizona Press, especially Allyson Carter, for your support and wonderful work with my project. I am grateful to the reviewers who provided thoughtful comments and guidance; their engagement with my work was invaluable. Several people gave advice and encouragement during the publication process: thanks Amy Lonetree, Andrea Smith, Nicole Guidotti-Hernandez, Karen Leong, Margaret Field, Ethel Nicdao, Laury Oaks, Beth Schneider, Sylvanna Falcón, Molly Talcott, Eva Garroutte, and Spero Manson. Thanks to my colleagues and mentors in the Native Elder Research Center Native Investigators Program for helping me develop as a scholar. Thanks to Kerry Ann Rockquemore and the NCFDD FSP community for loads of support. The Academic Ladder community also helped me grow as a writer. I am grateful to Judith Green for the wonderful *Yakama Rising* title idea. Finally, a big thank you to Chris and Anahuy, my favorite camping buddies. Áwna!

YAKAMA RISING

Introduction

Embodying Contradictions and Resisting Settler-Colonial Violence

An Ethnographic Introduction: Welcome Dance and Lessons Contained in Cultural Traditions

*   *   *

"There! Look," the grandmother said, nodding her head in the direction of the stage.

The woman follows the grandmother's gaze and smiles immediately. The children are dancing! On the stage are girls and boys dressed in their traditional regalia. They are so beautiful in their colorful outfits. She sees their advisor in the corner of the stage, announcing the next dance that the Wapato Indian Club dancers will perform. The woman takes in the scene and feels herself drift back in time, as a flood of memories washes over her.

In her memory, she sees a group of girls lined up in the large brick government building. There are cameras snapping photos, and it is a very crowded room. In the sea of people, she sees some familiar faces. She sees the watchful eyes of parents and the group's advisor, who expect a group of twenty girls to stand still while they wait for their introduction. She remembers trying to have proud, tall posture, as she had been taught by her auntie.

It was then that her older brother took the microphone. He was wearing the beaded vest that their auntie had made him. *Auntie is the most skilled seamstress in the entire world*, she thought to herself as she watched her brother make his introductory remarks. He was only thirteen years old, but the handsome vest made him seem mature beyond his age, she thought, *like a real spokesman for our people.* Finally, her brother finished his introduction of the opening dance. The girl and her nineteen friends took their cue and settled into a focused, but friendly, mood as they started the Welcome Dance.

The girls follow their lead dancer into the center of the room. They dance single file as they made the carefully timed and gentle steps with their feet. They keep pace with the drum and song, timing their steps with the graceful hand motions their elders had taught them in practice sessions.

In the dance, the girl gently places her hands in front of her body, then moves her wrists, rotating her palms upward. Then she turns her torso and moves her arms to extend her hands to the right, in a dramatic but gentle welcoming gesture to the guests to "sit here." She follows the lead dancer, keeps time with the drum, and repeats the motion, alternating to the left, letting the guests know they are also welcome to "sit there." All twenty girls dance in unison, with calm and proud expressions. They know it is an honor to open the ceremony today. Their dancing starts the event, and their elders taught them that having "good hearts" would establish the right mood and spirit, so the rest of the ceremony would go well. They knew these things, and embraced the responsibility, because their elders had prepared them for it. The Wapato Indian Club performance expressed the importance of a Yakama decolonizing praxis, as the girls embodied an ancient Yakama tradition of welcoming guests to an important event.

✳   ✳   ✳

Embodying Contradictions and Social Change: Yakama Cultural Revitalization on the Ground

This book examines Yakama cultural revitalization efforts as examples of healing the wounds of colonialism. Chapters 1, 2, and 3 each feature a case study highlighting dance, language, and food tradition revitalization, respectively; through these chapters, I introduce grassroots activists who share stories about the challenges and rewards of engaging in their community-building work. The women and men involved in the grassroots revitalization efforts recognize the importance of respecting women as culture bearers; therefore, each of the case studies is centered on

Yakama women elders' teachings. I argue that the activist work taking place is a powerful example of decolonization, and this book makes a contribution to the literature on indigenous social change by articulating a Yakama decolonizing praxis.

The dance event in the opening ethnographic narrative was a historical moment rich in meaning and contradiction. It was a celebration of the one-hundredth anniversary of Washington's statehood, an event that took place in 1989 at the grand opening of the newly built Washington State Department of Social and Health Services (DSHS) building. The large government structure was built on Yakama homeland, in the city of Yakima, named after our tribe, the Yakama Nation. Dignitaries from all levels of government attended, and the local news featured the event. At the time, it was probably difficult for us, a group of girls and boys from the nearby Yakama Reservation, to grasp the deeper significance. Our dancing represented an act of resisting colonialism, as we used our bodies to contest colonial logics that render indigenous peoples vanished, silent, and conquered.

Perhaps it is a fitting irony that Indian children danced to commemorate Washington's one-hundredth anniversary. Perhaps the dance reminded state officials of their obligation to our people. After all, the officials worked for a bureaucracy that existed as a result of the genocide and destruction of Indian peoples. Perhaps the display of dancing children and the presence of so many Indian bodies reminded officials that they were on Yakama homeland. Or, perhaps the audience simply saw, in amazement, that even after over one hundred years of the violence of colonization, settlement, war, and reservation policies, Yakama children could still take center stage at an official state event and steal the show. Yakama youth showed our pride, our humanity, our culture, and we became the teachers—as we embodied the knowledge that our elders had shared with us. In this way, our young bodies became a site of rich meaning and contradiction, where young indigenous people "talked back" to the state by demonstrating resistance to over a century of settler-colonial violence imposed upon our peoples. This book's case study of the youth dance troupe, together with case studies of language revitalization and traditional foods workshops, shares a compelling story of Native peoples working for change, while holding fast to our ancient traditions.

This tension, of working for change but holding onto traditions, is inherent within decolonization struggles. I use Waziyatawin and Michael Yellow Bird's definition of decolonization, "the intelligent, calculated, and active resistance to the forces of colonialism that perpetuate the subjugation and/or exploitation of our minds, bodies, and lands, and . . . is engaged for the ultimate purpose of overturning the colonial structure and realizing Indigenous liberation" (Wilson and Yellow Bird 2005, 5). Waziyatawin and Yellow Bird's definition provides an ideal toward which indigenous peoples are striving. Throughout the case studies in this book, I examine how decolonization efforts look "on the ground." I found that, ultimately, indigenous decolonization is about reclaiming traditions, in addition to moving forward in the complex social, political, and economic realities colonization brought to our peoples and homelands. Andrea Smith observed the dynamic approach that indigenous activists take in their decolonization efforts, stating it can be thought of as "revolution by trial and error" (Smith 2010b, 489). Negotiating the contradictions inherent in such change-making work is not always an easy process. Contemporary individuals and families negotiate the balance between pushing for change and understanding that not all peoples and institutions are ready for change. Through this uneasy process, activists seek alliances with those who support a decolonization agenda, and engage in what Smith calls, "identify[ing] possible nodal points of connection that can lead to global transformation" (Smith 2010a, 587). In the process of holding fast to traditions but working for change, activists create new methodologies to carry on traditional cultural practices. This transformative work is detailed in the case studies in chapters 1, 2, and 3, and they form the basis for what I call Yakama decolonizing praxis.

Growing up on the reservation, as an enrolled member of the Yakama Nation, I witnessed the contradictions inherent in efforts to hold fast to traditions yet work for social change. Now, as an ethnic studies professor, I examine such phenomena from a critical indigenous studies perspective, with the goal of supporting social change efforts that empower our people and protect our cultural traditions. My work to articulate a Yakama decolonizing praxis contributes to theories of indigenous social change centrally concerned with "making power" to reclaim indigenous traditions, bodies, languages, and homelands. These ongoing decolonizing efforts are needed because of the long history of struggle against settler-colonial violence that our people have endured.

Historical Background and Resisting Settler-Colonial Violence

According to tribal history, after contact with the infamous Lewis and Clark expedition in 1805 life "changed for us forever" (Yakima Indian

Nation Tribal Council 1977, 5). Our people extended friendship and welcomed the guests, as tradition requires. Ultimately the onslaught of settlers, territorial governments, and surveyors made it clear that these guests were not seeking to live peacefully among our people. Instead, they sought to take over our lands, subjugate our people and cultural ways, and colonize our institutions. When Washington Territory was formed in May 1853, Governor Isaac Stevens planned to resolve the "Indian problem" by entering into treaties with the indigenous peoples of what is now known as Washington State. Tribal historical accounts remember this time of tumultuous social change:

> Treaty plans called for lumping together these Indians living in this region. The majority of these Indians spoke dialects of the language now called Sahaptin. There were fourteen tribes and bands: the Palouse, Pisquouse, Wenatshapam, Klikatat, Klinquit, Kow-was-sayee, Li-ay-was, Skin-pah, Wish-Ham, Shyiks, Ochechotes, Kah-milt-pah, Se-ap-cat, and the Yakima.
> Over 3,000 Indian people and their leaders from the Yakima, Nez Perce, Umatilla, Walla Walla and Cayuse were called together in late May 1855 at Old Fort Walla Walla for the long and sometimes troubled treaty negotiations. (Yakima Indian Nation Tribal Council 1977, 9)

Ultimately, Yakama leaders were forced to sign the Treaty of 1855. Although 90 percent of Yakama homeland was ceded to the US government in this process, our Yakama leaders retained 1.2 million acres, which would be collectively held by our people and named the Yakama Reservation. Additionally, Yakama leaders fought to retain our traditional food gathering rights, and as a result we hold rights to fish, hunt, and gather in all the usual and accustomed places. Oral histories and tribal customs teach a great respect for our past leaders. In the words of Yakama leader Watson Totus, "Our hearts swell with praise for the dignity of our ancestors. We give respect to our forefathers who made our treaty. We try to walk today the path they made" (Yakima Indian Nation Tribal Council 1977, i).

Our leaders teach that, since time immemorial, Yakama peoples lived on our homeland, speaking the language provided to our people by the Creator and seeking to carry out the Original Teachings that the Creator provided. The name of our language, Ichishkíin, translates to "in this way," and elders remind younger learners that the language holds within it a powerful covenant between our people and the Creator. The language that the Creator bestowed upon us teaches us how to be; it teaches us how to conduct ourselves "in this way." Oral histories teach that the Creator made the land, all the plants, animals, and birds, and then the people (The Consortium of Johnson O'Malley Committees of Region IV State of Washington 1974). Tribal cultural committees have conducted projects to write down our people's oral histories, translating them into English, for modern-day convenience:

> In the beginning, our Creator spoke the word and this earth was created. He spoke the word again and all living things were put on the earth. And then He said the word and we, the (Indian) people, were created and planted here on this earth.
>
> We are like the plants of this earth. Our food was put here as plants to feed us; just like when we plant a garden. That is the way our earth was in the beginning.
>
> There were salmon, deer, elk, and all kinds of birds. It is as if our bodies are the very end of this earth, still growing while our ancestors are all buried in the ground.
>
> He named everything He created. He put water on this earth. He made it flow into the rivers and lakes to water this great garden and to quench the thirst of the people, the animals, plants, birds and fish.
>
> He took the feet of the people and made them walk on this earth. He created the horse; which is like a human being. He put the horse and the people together to help one another.
>
> All of the land where we live and where our ancestors lived was created for the (Indian) people. (Yakima Indian Nation Tribal Council 1977, 4)

Such oral histories tell about a Yakama view of history, of creation, and of the relationship between our people and our lands. As the lesson conveys, the land connects us to the Creator's original intention for our people, living, learning, and thriving on our homeland. The cultural revitalization efforts I discuss in this book are examples of our people building on these traditional teachings using contemporary methodologies. New methodologies are needed because of the dramatic social change that our people have faced. With each change introduced into our community, our people have had to make decisions about how to adapt and survive. As other scholars have detailed, this adaptation process is dynamic, complex, and at times contradictory.

Margaret Field and Paul Kroskrity write about the complications involved with indigenous language survival, acknowledging that "decisions about when to speak heritage and/or other languages in a community's linguistic repertoire and choices about whether to actively participate in language renewal efforts—or to assiduously avoid them—are prompted by *beliefs and feelings about language and discourse* that are possessed by speakers and their speech communities" (Field and Kroskrity 2009, 3–4). Such an observation calls attention to power dynamics that influence the survival of indigenous languages. As Teresa McCarty writes, "language choices are never unfettered, but rather play out within larger power regimes that structure individual agency and institutional constraints" (McCarty 2011, 9). Yakama children attending reservation schools, the growing importance of wage labor, and a general shifting of power toward the Western way of life were all evidence of the influence that the US government's assimilation policies has had on our people. Perhaps the most symbolic form of Western neocolonialism is The Dalles Dam, which was designed to destroy Celilo Falls, the most precious (and lucrative) salmon fishery for Indians in the Northwest. When the Army Corps of Engineers completed the massive Dalles Dam on March 10, 1957, the floodgates were closed, and the floodwaters buried Celilo Falls. The impact on the traditional Yakama economy was immediate and devastating, directly resulting in massive unemployment, dramatic increases in hunger and poverty, and unmeasured detriment to Yakama people's mental health and well-being (Hunn, and Selam and Family 1990; Barber 2005).

In her careful study of the social and political factors surrounding the construction of The Dalles Dam, Katrine Barber (2005) cites the numerous ways Yakama leaders protested the dam, noting in many cases how Yakama peoples provided the strongest examples of resistance. Yakama leaders paid their own expenses to travel to Washington, DC, to provide testimony against the construction of the dam. During one such visit, Watson Totus refused to give credence to the federal government's idea that a cash compensation would sufficiently reimburse Indians for the losses that the dam would impose. Totus stated that "no compensation could be made which would benefit my future generations, the people still to come" (Barber 2005, 86). Our leaders resisted the federal dam project because they foresaw how the dam would disrupt our traditional teachings and lifeways.

From an indigenous perspective, in order to care for the earth and our bodies, we must keep the traditional teachings alive. However, what happens when there is a knowledge gap? For example, when children have never touched a fresh salmon just pulled out of the river by our tribal fishermen? Or when children and adults are embarrassed to greet elders in our indigenous language? Or when children avoid or mock cultural gatherings because they have not learned the traditional dances? It is at these times, when cultural knowledge gaps are identified, that cultural revitalization becomes crucial. During times of cultural education crisis, activists must create new structures of teaching and learning, using what Denise Nadeau and Alannah Earl Young have described as an "Indigenous Knowledges framework" that includes traditional knowledge systems and practices as well as contemporary forms of knowledge that teach about "Indigenous theory, values, and cosmology, and provid[e] an embodied connection to relations" (Nadeau and Young 2008, 122–123). Or, as Joseph Gone (2010) describes in his community psychology framework, indigenous communities must draw from both traditional (precolonial) and contemporary (postcolonial) ways of reclaiming traditions and regenerating healthy communities. Thus, when younger generations are left with gaps in their knowledge of traditional cultural practices, activists respond by finding new ways of conceptualizing cultural revitalization work as they struggle to "seize the future" (Cornell et al. 2007) to ensure cultural survival.

Soul Wound and Indigenous Knowledge Production

Worldwide, indigenous peoples are struggling to protect their traditional cultural ways in the face of rapidly expanding Western consumer culture. Along with this struggle, indigenous peoples continue to face other threats, such as poor health, high poverty, low educational attainment, high suicide rates, and high rates of substance abuse. Lack of educational attainment is particularly worrisome among Native peoples, with US census data indicating Native peoples twenty-five years and older lag behind the general US population in high school graduation rates (76.6 percent vs. 85.0 percent) and bachelor's degree attainment (13.0 percent vs. 27.9 percent) (US Census Bureau 2010). These disparities contribute to a trend of lower earning power and job access among Native peoples. Within indigenous communities, the theory of intergenerational historical trauma and the concept of the soul wound are important tools for understanding the oppression of indigenous peoples (Duran 2006; Duran and Duran 1995).

Working as a counselor among Native peoples, Eduardo Duran found that community members had unresolved grief in response to the historical traumas their people had faced. For example, genocide, warfare, traditional homeland loss, forced attendance at boarding schools, and compulsory Christianity were all sources of grief and suffering for contemporary indigenous peoples. Duran found that indigenous peoples suffered with this grief even if they had not themselves directly experienced these forms of colonial violence. Adults whose parents were stolen by missionaries or government officials and taken to boarding schools, for example, often grieved over the violence and social disruption that occurred. Additionally, contemporary indigenous peoples experience post-traumatic stress disorder symptoms in response to historical events such as massacres of their tribal ancestors, forced treaty negotiations, cessation of tribal homelands, or removal and relocation of their tribal peoples.

Despite its popularity as an analytical tool among indigenous communities, historical trauma has been critiqued for perhaps defining indigenous peoples solely in terms of their relationship with colonizers, as Nadeau and Young (2008) articulate, and also for the lack of empirically based testing of historical trauma as a measurable concept (i.e., health scientists view historical trauma more as "folk knowledge" than a documented medical disorder, as Gone [2009] describes). However, the theoretical framework of historical trauma is still useful as a conceptual tool for understanding the long-term consequences of colonialism within contemporary indigenous communities from an indigenous perspective (as opposed to only a Western scientific perspective).

Community-based indigenous researchers continually engage the theory of historical trauma because of its strong appeal among indigenous communities themselves. Quite simply, indigenous communities engage with the theory because they find it helpful. Within this theoretical framework, the many social problems facing indigenous peoples are evidence of a traumatic response to colonial violence. As the theory explains, if the traumatic response to colonialism goes unaddressed and unresolved, then healing the soul wound will not happen. The trauma will worsen across generations. The soul wound is an important concept for decolonizing work because it accurately explains that the root cause of many social problems can be traced back to historical and ongoing forms of settler-colonial violence. Therefore, problems such as poverty, poor health, interpersonal violence, and substance abuse must be addressed within a framework that examines the long-term effects of colonialism. In so doing, scholars can actually avoid psychologizing Native peoples as "problems." In my work, I avoid the pitfalls of "stopping" the analysis at the soul wound and instead take it as an important jumping-off point to analyze the importance of developing a critical healing approach, in what I call Yakama decolonizing praxis. My analysis of Yakama cultural revitalization efforts contributes to indigenous studies theories that recognize the importance of our communities' resilience to understand and address our own problems—that the power needed to heal our soul wounds already exists within our people and traditions.

My concern with understanding suffering and resilience complements Dian Million's work in developing a "Felt Theory" that centers indigenous affect as central to indigenous feminist knowledge production. In Million's words, "Indigenous women participated in creating new language for communities to address the real multilayered facets of their histories and concerns by insisting on the inclusion of our lived experience, rich with emotional knowledges, of what pain and grief and hope meant or mean now in our pasts and futures" (Million 2009, 54). What ties the theoretical work on soul wound and felt theory together is the commitment to honor indigenous peoples' experiences and perspectives as central to a critical decolonized inquiry.

My study reveals that Yakama cultural revitalization activists have two interconnected goals: 1) recovering traditional cultural practices, and 2) dismantling oppressive systems that harm our people, land, and culture. The case studies that follow demonstrate how this Yakama decolonizing praxis looks. Through their everyday actions in and around the Yakama Reservation, in their travels to other institutions and gatherings, activists articulate a praxis that can inform feminist and anti-racist work. By drawing from traditions to undermine settler-colonial–imposed hierarchies and reasserting the importance of spiritual relations between humans and our surroundings, Yakama cultural revitalization efforts represent a distinctive indigenous feminist approach to "making power" within our community.

To address high rates of suicide and substance abuse, for example, one cannot simply look at problems in terms of an individual deficit or even as evidence of lack of sufficient available social services (although these realities can contribute to the problems as well). Rather, healing approaches must look at health and social problems in terms of land loss, genocide, warfare, assimilation, termination, and relocation. Likewise, indigenous peoples must view healing in terms of its long-term *communal* effects. To heal oneself is to help heal ancestors' soul wounds, and to help protect future generations from soul wound suffering. This view of healing and suffering resonates well with traditional indigenous teachings that view each generation as connected to another. Intergenerational historical trauma is a well-received theory within indigenous communities today because it centers the fact that suffering and healing are connected across generations; it reaffirms an indigenous belief in connectedness. As Native scholars note, it is difficult to imagine a contemporary indigenous health conference that does not address intergenerational historical trauma (Duran 2006; Evans-Campbell 2008). By taking up the notion of the soul wound, then, my analysis follows an important principle of decolonizing work: using indigenous communities' own ideas as central to an analysis that seeks to contribute to indigenous self-determination. This notion stands in contrast to a Western academic approach that assumes knowledge comes from "without" (or, "West is best," as Joseph Gone [2009] articulates in his critique). Linda Tuhiwai Smith points out that the strength of indigenous social movements "is to be found in the examples of how communities have mobilized locally, the grassroots development. It is at the local level that indigenous cultures and the cultures of resistance have been born and nurtured over generations. Successful initiatives have been developed by communities themselves using their own ideas and cultural practices" (Smith 2001, 110). Such perspectives start with an understanding of indigenous analyses as inherently valuable.[1]

Notably, resistance is taking place amid consistent attacks upon indigenous peoples' sovereignty, their cultural and physical existence. Brenda Child's work on understanding the boarding school experience points out that Native peoples have rich histories of resisting assimilationist policies and physical and structural violence. To do so, Native peoples draw from cultural traditions and look to their families and communities for support through emotional and cultural bonds (Child 1998).

This communal approach was important in the cases of Yakama cultural revitalization I share in this book. Faced with the daunting reality that the survival of Yakama cultural traditions were at stake, cultural revitalization activists worked together to build movements that would ensure the younger generations have access to their cultural teachings.

My study of Yakama cultural revitalization contributes to the ongoing discussion of decolonization within indigenous studies by helping to fill an important gap: I ground my analysis within specific case studies of decolonization movements taking place within a particularly under-researched community, which also happens to be the largest tribe in the Northwest. By looking at what activists are doing, documenting their history and impact, we can understand how decolonization, as a practice, helps inform our theory-building of decolonization and social change.

---

[1]Stuart Kirsch makes a similar argument in his work with indigenous peoples in New Guinea, arguing for the value of a "reverse anthropology" that privileges indigenous modes of analysis (Kirsch 2006).

The models of grassroots activism I outline and discuss in this book have already served our community well. But there is more work to be done. Within our own community, activists acknowledge that more people need to be involved in revitalization efforts—that the movement needs to grow stronger. Indeed, as a critical indigenous scholar, I agree that our decolonization work must continue because, ultimately, our traditions and languages will not be fully restored until global transformation abolishes the multiple forms of oppression that perpetuate the physical and cultural genocide of indigenous peoples. Beyond our Yakama community, this book will provide guidance to other peoples who seek to bring about healing social change. Today, so many communities feel a great need for healing. We will all benefit when we learn from each other, share our successes, analyze our common problems, and nurture and support the optimism and courage that serve as the foundation of our movements.

Methods

In 2010–2011, I conducted qualitative interviews with eighteen people involved in three case studies of cultural revitalization movements on the Yakama Reservation. These case studies focus on dance (Wapato Indian Club), language (Northwest Indian Language Institute), and food (X̱wayamamí Ishích), respectively. I used a snowball sampling technique, starting with key personnel for each case study. As a member of the Yakama Nation and a community member active within cultural revitalization efforts, I was familiar with some of the work being done through these grassroots efforts, but I had not previously analyzed or written about this cultural revitalization work. I loosely structured interviews, asking each interviewee about their experiences, motivations, and advice for future generations (see Appendix).

In addition, I asked each interviewee if they considered themselves to be an "activist," as I was interested in whether they viewed their work as explicitly activist in nature. As Winona LaDuke points out, labels such as "activist" or "feminist" are embraced in indigenous communities depending on who is doing the defining (LaDuke 2005a). As I discuss in later chapters, elders were most accepting of an "activist" label or identity, while younger interviewees shied away from what they perceived might be a "strong" or "political" association connected with an activist label. It appeared the younger respondents' hesitation to embrace an activist title was rooted in humility, a point I discuss further in chapter 3. For example, younger people framed their work in terms of "just helping" elders, who were the *real* activists. Regardless of their political differences in embracing various labels, there was one striking similarity across all interviewees: deep concern for "Native survivance," as termed by Gerald Vizenor. Native survivance focuses on an active presence and the continuation of stories within Native communities, a point discussed in greater detail in chapter 2 (Vizenor 2008).

During the informed consent process, each participant was offered anonymity and the use of a pseudonym, but all participants chose to have their real names used in this study. Interviews, on average, were 45 minutes long, audiotaped, transcribed verbatim, coded, and analyzed for themes. All the quotes in the case studies come from these interviews unless otherwise indicated and, along with my own reflections, informed the ethnographic descriptions included in this book. The inclusion of researcher reflection is considered a strength, as researcher reflexivity is an important part of the analytical process (Jacob 2006; McGhee, Marland, and Atkinson 2007; Smith 2002).

Overview of Chapters

The Wapato Indian Club youth group was formed in the 1970s, in response to student demand that cultural teachings be present within the public school. Students urged their school counselor to help them learn the teachings. Their counselor, a Yakama woman, reached out to elders, and they began the work. Some forty years later the club is still going strong, its performances being sought by venues across the United States. This chapter shares the lessons that club alumni, elders, and club advisors learned over the course of the club's history. In chapter 1, I study how the dances themselves became an educational tool to help children embody the teachings of their elders. Focusing on one particular dance, the Swan Dance, I analyze the cultural lessons contained within the actual technique and spirit of the dance. I conclude the chapter with a Yakama-specific set of values that articulates the leadership model which underlies the work of the Wapato Indian Club.

Chapter 2 focuses on a group of activists who resist the extinction of the indigenous Yakama language, Ichishkíin. The language revitalization movement, led by a Yakama woman elder, evolved into a partnership with the University of Oregon's Northwest Indian Language Institute (NILI). In the chapter, I study the ways activists utilize a vision of social justice to build what linguists have called a moral community. Inherent within this approach is the understanding that indigenous peoples possess a human right to learn and use their languages. In addition, contemporary educational institutions have a responsibility to respond to and protect this right. This chapter articulates the educational model that garnered successful results for these activists.

Down a bumpy dirt road in a remote area of the reservation, there is education taking place. It is advertised on Facebook and through word of mouth. Generations of Yakama families gather to learn the traditional food ways of our people. The teacher, a tribal elder, drives several hours from her home near the Columbia River to show the younger people how to wind-dry fish, a traditional way of preserving food that does not rely on electricity or artificial preservatives. This is one example of the work done within X̱wayamamí Ishích (Golden Eagle's Nest), a community-based nonprofit organization dedicated to cultural revitalization on the Yakama Reservation. In chapter 3, I draw from in-depth interviews and participant observation to analyze the importance of the activists' work, paying special attention to their traditional foods workshops. I also analyze the way their work represents an important example of grassroots indigenous resistance with the potential to dismantle colonial logics. I conclude the chapter by articulating a model of education that underlies their work.

Chapter 4 discusses the larger lessons drawn from across the case studies by incorporating my work on historical trauma with the literatures of Native feminism, indigenous resurgence, and indigenous human rights. In doing so, I discuss the importance of women elder–centered indigenous social change and the emergence of a Yakama decolonizing praxis. I discuss the activists' successes, as well as their shared cautionary advice about the political tensions and contradictions involved in doing cultural revitalization work. The stakes of indigenous grassroots activism, and the unlimited potential of such work, underlie the importance of Yakama decolonizing praxis, which has three main characteristics: 1) understanding indigenous bodies as sites of critical pedagogy, 2) centering social justice praxis to build a moral community, and 3) utilizing grassroots indigenous resistance as a mechanism to dismantle colonial logics.

Chapter 5 provides an outline of the steps needed to further institutionalize the examples of Yakama decolonizing praxis revealed in the case studies. This next step is necessary in a time when all peoples need healing education in our schools and communities, as all people have inherited the legacy of colonialism. The essence of the chapter reflects a point activists made and remade during their interviews: despite their many accomplishments, they are ordinary people just trying to do the best they can, all the while insisting that *anyone* could do cultural revitalization work. Anyone can join in the work to recover and revitalize indigenous traditions and bring about radical social change to create power within indigenous communities. This profound point, insisting that anyone can do this work, represents the spirit of the activists' work: humble, practical, strong, determined, and clever. All of the activists I interviewed urge more people to help with this work—to share ideas and grow the movement bigger and better. Chapter 5 fittingly provides recommendations for academics and indigenous community members who would like to take up the activist call articulated in this book.

These summaries provide the outline of the journey this book offers. I hope you enjoy the places, people, and the exciting forms of social change shared in the stories this book contains. I hope the narratives of the activists, the complexities they face, and the strong spirit of their work inspires you to think deeply about ways that all people can benefit from healing social change rooted in a decolonizing agenda.

CHAPTER ONE

Teach Them in a Good Way

Critical Pedagogy of the Wapato Indian Club

The Body as a Site for Critical Pedagogy:
An Ethnographic Introduction

✳   ✳   ✳

The schoolchildren smile, giggle, and chat excitedly, filling the concrete locker rooms with a loud, happy murmur. They open their suitcases and begin dressing in their regalia, most students careful not to muss their hair, which family members or friends had carefully braided earlier in the day, before school or during the lunch period. One girl is not so careful, pulling the layers of clothes quickly over her head. She is dressed first, and is thinking about how she can perhaps race to the bus, beating all of the other children, and grab the most coveted seat, the bench in the far back. As she clicks her suitcase closed, surveys how slowly all the other girls are dressing, one of her friends suspects her plan to be first on the school bus, and tries to squash her plan. "Ha ha! Your braids are all fuzzy! Look!" her friend blurts out, pointing and trying to get other girls to join in teasing their quick-dressing friend. The quick dresser pauses a moment, wondering if she really did have fuzzy braids, or if her friend is just trying to slow her down in an effort to win the coveted back seat. Enough doubt fills her mind that she scampers over to the locker room mirror, sliding on the cement floor in her leather-soled moccasins. *Darn!* She *had* been too quick. Her braids are all fuzzy, and the smooth part her mother made this morning now has several loose hairs flying about in the static of the reservation's dry air. She wonders what she should do. Using the locker room mirror, she scans the room behind her. Other girls are already clicking their suitcases shut, and she will lose all hope of a good seat on the bus if she rebraids her hair. She decides to settle on a quick fix. She runs her hand under the cold water faucet and smoothes out the part down the middle of her head. *There, that is good enough*, she thinks. In the bus she will cover her braids with *nuksháy* (otter fur) anyway, *so who cares if they are fuzzy*, she justifies to herself silently. Feeling better about her appearance, she smiles a little at herself in the mirror. She takes a moment and looks at the beautiful beaded dress she wears, her grandmother's dress, which was gifted to her this year when her parents honored her for choosing to participate in the dance group at her middle school.

Eventually, all the children, both girls and boys, load on the bus and greet their favorite school bus driver. Their advisor watches them kindly but sternly, to make sure the teasing and playing does not get out of hand. Once boarded, they make their way to the highway, off the reservation, to the city named after their tribe. The children feel delighted that, of all the Wapato Indian Club members, they were chosen to go on this field trip during the school day. Their hard work—attending club meetings and dance practices, and having good grade reports from their teachers—had paid off. On the bus ride, they speak about classes they are especially glad to miss, just quiet enough to be out of earshot of their advisors, or so they thought. Once at the venue, all the children crowd out of the bus, excited to be at the event. The advisor gathers the group together before entering the large new brick building. She hushes them with a wave of her hand, and then explains that they are now cultural ambassadors representing the school, the community, and the tribe. She reminds them that she expects their best behavior in front of their audience. The children listen quietly, respectfully. One parent, who is attending as a chaperone, marvels that the advisor can quiet forty middle school children with a motion of her hand.

*　　*　　*

Indigenizing the Educational System: Elders, Swans, and Cultural Teachings

The Wapato Indian Club was formed in 1973, as a result of student demands to have a place within their public school where Indian identities were affirmed and nurtured. At the time, the school district had no curricular or extracurricular activities focused on American Indian culture or history. The club persists because of the belief that it offers something unique and necessary to the children who take part in its activities, as children learn to use their bodies to express their cultural identities and to honor the teachings of their elders. This chapter shares an emerging theory of indigenous social change that is based on qualitative interviews with current and former Wapato Indian Club advisors, club alumni, and their parents.

In this chapter, I argue that the activist education taking place within the Wapato Indian Club helps us understand the body as a site of critical pedagogy. The educational process used in the Wapato Indian Club is an example of how indigenous peoples are reshaping educational institutions to move from dependence to autonomy. The Wapato Indian Club case study demonstrates the power of applying an indigenous pedagogy—as children involved with the club learn a "way of being" that promotes cultural pride, a critical understanding of cultural identity, and a sense of self that is rooted in elders' teachings. Because of its grounded approach, my analysis of the club's indigenous pedagogy and the articulation of an embodied cultural revitalization process is a contribution to the existing literature on indigenous social change.

The story of the Wapato Indian Club is one of students gaining voice in expressing the importance of a critical indigenous pedagogy. But how did a group of Indian students find a way to create space for indigenous cultural revitalization within the public school system? They approached the only Yakama counselor who worked in the district, Sue Rigdon, a strong woman who cares about the community and her students. In reflecting on the founding of the club, Sue smiled as she remembered how the students "kept pestering" her to teach them. The students trusted that she would respond to their needs to be more connected to their culture. The students were interested in dancing, and they believed that Sue, out of all the people they knew, would be the one person who could help form the Wapato Indian Club dance group.

Sue took her responsibility to the children very seriously, because if they were craving these cultural teachings, then she should make an effort to help them. Sue did what traditional cultural teachings instruct: seek out mentorship from tribal elders. She stated: "I [went to see] Hazel Miller. She taught us, no she didn't teach, she *told* us about the dances. Each one has a spirit and its own life. You danced to that." In her interview, Sue related how elders began instructing her by telling her about the dances, to ensure that Sue understood the background and meaning of the dances or, as Sue more eloquently states, the "spirit" of each dance. In this way, the elders were sharing the lessons that they themselves had learned through the oral tradition.

Perhaps one of the reasons Sue was so understanding and generous in teaching the dances to the children in the Wapato Indian Club is because she shared a strong common bond with them. The Wapato Indian Club served as a common vehicle through which they all learned some aspects of Indian cultures. During the planning stages of this book project, I met with Sue numerous times to review documents and to finalize my interview guides. In our discussions, she shared with me that it was important to ask interviewees whether they had known the dances before they participated in the club, or if they, like Sue, learned the dances as a result of being part of the Wapato Indian Club. Sue was always known as a strong role model for the students, including the way she demonstrated humble leadership by never acting as if she knew things she did not. As written elsewhere, it is important within traditional Yakama culture that leaders do not assert authority for its own sake (Jacob and Peters 2011). Strong Yakama leaders are accountable to the people and humble in their positions of authority, only asserting authority when called to do so by the people. This cultural teaching is what served as the foundation for Sue's leadership within the Wapato Indian Club, as she worked with students, their families, and the school administration to found the club and begin teaching traditional dances.

Sue's humble leadership and caring manner helped her understand the feelings of the children who yearned to learn the dances. Sue shared stories about her own childhood, and she shared that her family, like many indigenous families, had struggled with alcoholism. Because of this, she was raised by her elderly and disabled grandmother, who was unable to teach Sue the dances and was physically challenged to attend events where Sue could watch and participate. Thus, Sue did not learn the dances as a youth. A generation later, when Sue was recruited to be the school counselor in the 1970s, she worked with a younger generation who had similar backgrounds. For various reasons, many of the students had a gap in knowledge; they had not learned the traditional dances at home, or they wanted a deeper knowledge of them. Thus, when the students insisted that Sue help teach them the traditional dances, she humbly sought mentorship from elders. Sue took the time to learn the dance traditions from elders so that she could provide that education for the young people who wanted to learn. Thus, by filling her own knowledge gap, Sue was empowered to make a great contribution to intergenerational teaching and learning. Her work to revitalize and share these cultural teachings connected the young people with the elders' teachings.

One of the first elders who worked with her was Hazel Miller, an important teacher who provided oral histories and instruction about the dances, which Sue took back to the Wapato Indian Club students. Sue's involvement in founding the Wapato Indian Club had, at its core, a healing component. By reaching out on behalf of the schoolchildren, Sue learned the traditions so she could share them with the younger generations. Such action represents a step toward healing the soul wound that alcoholism, a destructive response by indigenous peoples to colonialism, had inflicted (Brave Heart 1999, 2003; Brave Heart and DeBruyn 1998; Evans-Campbell 2008; Duran 2006). Sue's work to learn the lessons and teach them to the schoolchildren healed not only Sue, but also the schoolchildren who wanted to learn the lessons, either more deeply than they had learned at home, or for the first time.

Sue carefully noted that Hazel *told* about the dances, sharing the background and meaning of the dances and providing stories that go with each dance. Sue listened carefully to the elder and then started taking that knowledge back to the Wapato Indian Club practices, sharing that cultural knowledge and engaging in the teaching of the dances to students, through rigorous repetition, during group practices. To help with this work of teaching the dances, Sue had to reach out to other elders and adults who then began attending the dance practices, demonstrating, instructing, drumming, and singing to help the children learn. As the advisor for the club, Sue felt a special honor and obligation to teach the students to respect the traditions that the elders shared with the younger generations. Sue emphasizes that she was taught by the elder that each dance has a "spirit and its own life." Thus, learning to do the traditional dances is a spiritual act, as dancers must learn to represent the spirit of the dance, to become one with it. When discussing the dances, she describes this transformation of people, songs, and the spirit of the dance. An example is the Swan Dance, a dance that is held special in Yakama tradition and has been performed countless times across our homeland. Therefore, teaching the younger generations about the dance connects the youth to a proud tradition of our people and land. The dance connects the dancers and their audiences to a sacred being, the Swan. Legends connect the Swan Dance to the Lake Chelan area in Washington State, and the dance creates bonds across generations of Plateau peoples, who share in the tradition of looking to the gifts of the Creator for important lessons about how to conduct oneself. Sue said:

> The girls' Swan Dance, the dance is beautiful . . . To honor the swan bird, it really is pretty when they dance it. They go up and then they go down, and then they go up and then they go down. You know, like a swan, and then they come to the circle and they chatter to each other. And they go up and they go around again and they dance off. And it is really pretty. It is an honor, an offering to the swan bird who flies through the air with such grace and beauty.

The words that Sue uses to describe the dance include *beautiful, honor, pretty, offering, grace,* and *beauty.* Sue shares that the dance is an honor offered to the swan, that the girls who learn and perform this dance are offering respect to the bird. As offerings are a form of prayer, the girls are providing an offering of respect, grace, and beauty.

Such an offering serves as a blessing: to the bird, to the girls who are performing the dance, to the audience participating as witnesses to this offering, to the elders who carry on the teachings and share them with the girls, and to the ancestors who are part of the legacy of the traditional dances. This way of relating to the living beings of our homeland, to all of creation around oneself, is a holistic way of viewing the world. It represents an indigenous view of a good education. As such, the swan plays an important role in my analysis of the Wapato Indian Club, which I discuss further with figure 2.

Sue roots her description of the Swan Dance and its meaning within a spiritual realm. It is not simply a dance *about* a bird. Nor is it simply a dance to *imitate* a bird. Rather, it is an honoring of the bird. It is an offering to the bird, who is a beautiful part of creation on our homeland. In this way, the Wapato Indian Club provides a cultural teaching, which is rooted in place-based spirituality. Yet, being associated with a public school, this aspect of spirituality, which Westerners often conflate with "religion," is not emphasized in public descriptions of the club's activities. However, the club certainly is known for teaching and sharing cultural lessons of Yakama peoples and a broader pan-Indian culture as well. For example, in a newspaper article about the club's invited performance at a national musician's conference in San Diego, a Wapato school board member voiced her support for the trip, saying the Indian Club students "will be goodwill ambassadors for Wapato. I can't think of a better way to show people who we are" ("Board authorizes Indian Club trip" 1991). The goodwill message of the dancers touched audiences. Sue recalled, during her interview with me: "People cried every time we performed." Additionally, Sue explained in a newspaper article that when the club performs, "It's an opportunity to provide truly intercultural understanding" ("The Past Is the Future" 1993). Such lessons, rooted in an indigenous-centered educational model, provide audiences with a gift. Audiences are overwhelmed by the generosity and beauty of the young dancers and, as Sue notes, were brought to tears.

Dances accomplish several important functions. They affirm the importance of the oral histories and traditional cultural lessons that elders teach; they affirm the importance of the girls who are dedicated to learning these lessons and carrying on the traditions. They affirm the importance of the audiences, who witness and honor the girls and the traditions. And, at a fundamental level, the dances teach—they instruct—Yakama peoples how to live and what should be valued. The Swan Dance teaches the value of unity, as the girls embody working together in unison, and of individuals falling into an order that is collectively greater than any individual. It teaches followers to be aware of the leader, and teaches the leader to be aware of the followers. All participants are crucially important, and a specific kind of unison is needed in order to do the dance in a way that represents the traditional teachings that elders share. The Swan Dance also teaches the importance of having fun, of being social. As Sue stated, "they come into the circle and they chatter to each other."

The girls demonstrate that they can carry out precision and unity as a group; leader and followers working together are one strong, beautiful, and graceful collective. However, at a special time during the dance, the drumbeat escalates and the girls break out of their single file order and rush to the middle, coming together again as one with their hands fluttering and chattering friendly and excited noises. This is a playtime, a time of laughing and smiling; it is the time when they relax, cheer, and joke. Then, at the appointed time, the drumbeat signals to them that the playtime is over, they need to transition back into their single-file order, backing gently out of the chattering group, the girls again take up motions in unison, bowing gently to each strong drumbeat, until they are back in their original order and performing the graceful actions of diving swans.

The lesson inherent in this part of the dance is that our people must take time to laugh and have fun, to loosen up the strict order and discipline of a precise group, to smile and giggle. Then the transition takes place where the group must, again, regain order and the leaders must be strong, attentive, and proud. Followers must carry out their responsibilities to the group. The followers have a special role in this dance, as they are whom the audience will see most. There are few leaders, and many followers. The leaders must be strong, predictable, and patient, able to change what they are doing (whether pacing slower or faster, or changing the path that the group will take) if that is what is best for the overall unison of the group.

Indigenous Education in Practice:
An Ethnographic Reflection

*   *   *

As a youth, I remember being called into Sue's office. A hall pass had arrived for me, excusing me from my regular class time, because I was required to visit the counselor's office. Walking down the industrial-carpeted and fluorescent-lit hallway, I make the familiar trek to Sue's office. It was a popular hangout for Native students. We'd go in to receive a kind smile or just to say hello, or to drop off something that perhaps a family member had sent for Sue, a returned borrowed item, or a small gift to thank her for her generosity with the youth. It is a space where we knew we would be accepted, respected, and encouraged. With the door open, I walk into Sue's small office, which is cluttered with mementos from adoring students, parents, and community members. I am surprised to see one of my best friends there.

After the flash of surprise, I begin to worry. I can feel my brow furrow and I give my friend a nervous glance. It was unusual for two students to be pulled out of class at the same time for a meeting.

We all greet each other quietly, and then Sue waits a moment before she calmly looks at us and says she is disappointed. We, a couple of the strongest leaders in the club, have been very cliquish lately, she tells us. We weren't including all the students in our activities, and we acted like we didn't care about the whole group.

Stunned and ashamed, we knew Sue's words were true. I feel my cheeks beginning to sting with embarrassment. I think through the past couple of weeks and realize that we had indeed been bratty middle-school kids lately, letting our sarcasm, eye-rolling, and note-passing get out of hand.

We stare quietly at the ground, nervous and embarrassed. After a moment of silence, we mumble apologies to our advisor. After a serious moment, she clears the air, as she smiles and reminds us how important we are. We know her words are genuine, as we can see the kindness in her dark brown eyes. She lifts our spirits by telling us we are role models to the other students. She tells us to be more inclusive of all students, to spend time talking and sharing with the other students, and to remember that we are responsible to the whole group.

Soaking up her instructive words, we nod our heads in agreement and promise to do a better job. She reminds us of the responsibility and dedication that we need to show as leaders. "That is the way of our people," she reminds us on a serious note.

After the serious talk, we turn to lighter topics; we talk about the new recycling program taking place at the school. We admire the snapshot photos that someone's parent had recently brought for Sue. We talk about how our families are doing and the results of the latest sports team competition. After we enjoy our small talk, Sue asks us if we are ready to go back to class.

"I guessssssssss," we moan, pretending that we don't like school, although we are both pretty dedicated students. She writes us the necessary hall passes and we leave, exchanging smiles and soft handshakes or hugs on our way out the door.

After we think we are out of earshot, we share some candy and gum, of course against the school rules, and we roll our eyes about being called cliquish. But deep down, underneath these adolescent defense mechanisms, we know Sue is right. She is our most treasured role model at the middle school. We love spending time with her and we know she would never steer us astray. We both silently agree that we will try to do better; we will try harder to live up to Sue's expectations. We know that her teachings are important, but it would take years, even decades, for us to more fully reflect on exactly how important these teachings are, to realize the gift that she is sharing with us.

*　　*　　*

Articulating a Critical Indigenous Pedagogy

In our interview, I asked Sue about the important lessons that the children would learn through their participation in the Wapato Indian Club. She explained the multiple layers of education that took place, and that student empowerment is a main goal:

I always have a way with teaching. We had fun, you know, we did things that are fun. But when it comes to teaching the dance, I want them to be respectful of what I am giving them. And I want them to be good at it, so when they show it to other people, they will know and they will be proud.

Here we gain insight into the way Sue approached teaching the traditional dances to the children. There are four parts to the pedagogy that she describes.

First, because she is working with children, the foundation of the work must be fun. Without that foundation, the children would lose interest and group members would probably have difficulty bringing a "good heart" to the practices and performances. This is a powerful message from which other activists can learn: decolonizing work can be stressful— challenging the entrenched ways of settler colonialism and its imposition on our lives. Yet, Sue reminds us that activism must allow for fun. Sue's narrative illustrates that important principles of decolonization include having fun, to ensure sustainability, while also holding high standards and expectations of those involved.

Second, she wants students to understand that, in sharing the teachings of the dances, Sue is providing them with a gift. A main teaching within traditional culture is that one must acknowledge that receiving a gift is an honor, and that one must be respectful of both the gifts received and the gift giver, who is honoring the one receiving the gift. Gifts serve an important function within Yakama culture. They bring relations together in a cycle of reciprocity. When a child joins the Wapato Indian Club, they are entering into that set of relations where they need to learn to be respectful of the teachings and honorable toward all of the other participants: teachers, elders, past performers, current performers, future performers, audience members, community, and school officials. This elaborate set of relations is nurtured and sustained through efforts to teach about the traditions of giving, receiving, and honoring each other.

Third, students must dedicate themselves to learn the dances and to perform them well. This emphasis on achievement is important, because it would be disrespectful to perform the dances poorly, or to demonstrate a lack of discipline to learn the dances. Sue had high standards, expecting perfection, or close to it, and the students were expected to hold these same expectations for themselves and their classmates. Sue's insistence on high-quality performances and a respectful dedication to learning traditions is indicative of her awareness of the stakes of cultural revitalization.

If the work is done sloppily or without great respect, then the impact and social change potential of their work will also be diminished, rendering their decolonizing efforts fruitless.

Fourth, students must be high achievers, because they are serving as ambassadors to their audiences. They must perform the traditional dances in a way that proudly represents the Yakama people, American Indians, and the students themselves. Sue describes the fourth part of the teaching process as one that focuses on self-esteem. In her view, the children must do great performances so the audiences will know—and more important, so the children will know—that they have done a good job. The children must feel pride in learning and sharing the traditional dances. This part of the teaching process would not be possible without the other three parts, and I argue that this final part of the process is perhaps the most important—in terms of preparing club members for future grassroots activist work and continuing the cultural revitalization process that Sue helped them learn.

Within the Yakama context, self-esteem differs from the Western notion. Saying the Wapato Indian Club helped students' individual self-esteem would be an understatement. It would gloss over much of the richness and possibility that we can learn from this example. In the typical Western view, positive self-esteem is about a favorable belief in oneself as an individual. However, in analyzing Sue's narrative, Yakama self-esteem goes beyond the individual. The collective ethos marks the concept of self-esteem, as it does with Yakama traditions more generally. For Sue, the self-esteem of the Wapato Indian Club members is rooted in the dedication, discipline, and pride that the children feel as part of a collective that is learning and living the traditional teachings. The children feel pride, in Sue's ideal vision of the teaching process, because they have done a good job sharing their knowledge of the dances, and the children feel good about knowing they have shared with and taught their audiences. They feel good because they can be counted on as culture bearers, even at their young ages, as Sue explained:

> I tell them when they come in to join us, that they are joining a club that is fun, but it is different. They are coming to learn about the Indian culture. And it's very proud. And they must treat it with respect.

Sue reiterates the main points of the teaching process that I shared in this section. She emphasizes that fun is important, as with all the other youth clubs, but that the Wapato Indian Club is different. Within the club, the most important thing is to learn about Indian culture. She mentions that the culture is very proud, signaling that she expects a serious commitment from the students, that casual participation will not be enough to learn the lessons adequately. She finishes her statement by saying that the students *must* treat the cultural lessons with respect. Anything else but committed, serious learning will not be tolerated. The club cannot afford to have the cultural teachings disrespected in that way. Again, this is part of Sue's responsibility as an elder who has herself been gifted these teachings by her elders. If she allows these teachings to be disrespected, then it brings a dishonor to the other students, to the community, to Sue, to the elders who gifted the teachings to Sue, and to the student who fails to follow the rules within this indigenous-centered education. If Sue does not uphold that traditional cultural value in her teachings, then she will not successfully teach the students perhaps the most important lesson, of respecting the cultural teachings and their elders. The pedagogy of the Wapato Indian Club can be understood as an example of what Sandy Grande describes as critical pedagogy. Grande states: "'critical pedagogy' operates in the educational landscape as both a rhetoric and a social movement" (Grande 2004, 6). Sue's efforts to instill in the children a sense of pride in their heritage and responsibility to their community provides youth with a message and example of how to work toward social justice and decolonization, which are the purposes of critical pedagogy (Grande 2004).

While a main purpose of the Wapato Indian Club, from its founding, was to help pass on traditional teachings and dances to Indian youth, the club also honored a multicultural vision that welcomed interested and committed non-Native students into the club. Natalie Curfman was one such club participant, who was active in the Wapato Indian Club during all three years of her middle-school attendance in the late 1980s and early 1990s and was elected by her fellow club members to serve as a club officer. In her interview, Natalie emphasized a major lesson that she learned through her involvement with the club:

> I think the thing that I appreciated most is that Sue included people like me. I am Caucasian. I'm not Native American, but to me the club was important because Wapato is my community, too. I feel like culture is where you live. I think that was the biggest gift. Sue was willing to share cross-culturally . . . I really felt that it was a gift, something to appreciate growing up. It helps you to be more flexible in different senses . . . working with people who are different than you . . . I certainly hope that the club would continue because I

think it is helping to keep the heritage of Yakama people alive, for one thing, and having pride in the culture, but also the chance at cross-cultural experiences are important, to help people like me.

Natalie reflects on her experience as a non-Native member of the Wapato Indian Club and refers to it as a gift that she continues to carry with her. She mentions that it helped her to learn to be flexible and it taught her valuable cross-cultural skills. She credits Sue's generosity in sharing Yakama teachings; Natalie was encouraged to seek these teachings out because she, too, was part of the Wapato community on the Yakama Reservation. She honors the fact that Sue gifted her with teachings that helped her have a more meaningful connection to Yakama peoples and homeland. Natalie's experience helps demonstrate that an indigenous-centered educational experience can benefit non-indigenous students.

Yakama Reservation community members speak of the Wapato Indian Club as providing guidance that youth, and their families, need. It provides a safe space for Indian and non-Indian children to learn about Indian cultures. For Native students, it validates the importance and pride in having an Indian identity. Margaret Carter, a teacher at the Wapato Middle School and current Wapato Indian Club advisor, also discussed cultural pride in terms of intergenerational teaching and learning, as club alumni stay involved with the club and mentor the younger students through learning the dances and perfecting their performances. For example, she mentioned that middle-school children who are just starting to learn the dances could sometimes be "shy" or "nervous" during performances. She explained that club alumni hold the children to high standards, knowing the children are representing the larger community when they do their performances:

> They come back and teach the little kids and perform with us. It is a strong tie; it's like they want to stay in the family, which is fine with me! Because the older ones, they are the ones, too, who will say "Hey you need to quit playing around out there." They are actually more strict than I am, as far as the performance level. I'll be like, "Well, they are just a little shy." They'll say, "No! they need to quit fidgeting." But that's good, because it is teaching them leadership also. You become a leader when you're out there.

Margaret's narrative describes the characteristics of good leadership within the Wapato Indian Club. Alumni and advisors help younger performers overcome feelings of shyness or nervousness so they can reach their full potential as proud leaders of the club, and ultimately as representatives of the Yakama people and homeland. On the reservation, very few youth leadership opportunities exist; there are no Boys & Girls Clubs or YMCA on the reservation, and local parks and recreation departments offer infrequent programming. The Wapato Indian Club represents a valuable opportunity to teach young people leadership skills and to do so in a way that centers the importance of Native identity, culture, and representation, as defined by reservation community members. As such, it is a leadership training program that takes place on Yakama homeland with the intent of building strong leaders who are comfortable representing where they are from in a way that is proud, dignified, and respectful. The fact that alumni return to the club to work with younger children is evidence that the club's message is effective. Alumni, who instruct the young children to "quit playing around" on stage, help reinforce the message to youth that their actions matter and the community relies on the youth to be a proud representation of our people and homeland.

Identity, Culture, and Resisting Negative Stereotypes

Interviewees discussed the variety of dances that the Wapato Indian Club performed, including traditional Yakama dances, such as the Swan Dance and the Welcome Dance, and what they referred to as powwow-style dances, such as the Grass Dance and Sneak Up Dance. Such forms of cultural expression are obviously rooted in indigenous traditions. Yet, powwow is understood as a contemporary pan-Indian cultural tradition. The inclusion of powwow dancing as part of the Wapato Indian Club pedagogy confirmed that identity is fluid, rather than fixed. The group could perform a Plateau dance, such as the Swan Dance, and in the next moment perform a Plains-style Grass Dance. These teachings helped students understand the flexibility of identity and gave students the opportunity to learn that being comfortable with contradictions was also important in forming a strong Yakama identity. This teaching is perhaps most evident with regard to the club's sign language performances. The sign language numbers were performed in unison, with the children wearing their full traditional regalia, to musical renditions that were played via audio system by tape or CD. All of the performances, including the dances and sign language routines, were taught to the children and advisors by elders, including the sign language routine of the Lord's Prayer. Sue mentioned that, at times, audience members might question whether the sign language numbers were "really traditional." Sue's response was that if an elder had gifted it to her to share with the children, then it became part of the Wapato Indian Club tradition.

In the mid-1990s, the Wapato Indian Club began selling self-published booklets about their performance numbers, as a fundraiser to support their travel and regalia-making costs. Within the booklet entitled "Wapato Indian Club: Traditional Dances and Stories of the Yakama Indian Nation," there is an explanation of the different performance numbers that the club would typically perform. On the cover of the booklet (see figure 1), there is a drawing of two dancers signing part of the Lord's Prayer. The booklet included the following explanation of sign language performances:[1]

> The first people of this land, which came to be known as America, were diverse in language and social customs. Being extremely separate, yet mobile societies, the effort to communicate necessitated the use of sign language. Our Wapato Indian Club performers do a variety of northern and southern Indian sign language. Much of the American deaf sign language is adapted from American Indian sign language. Some of the numbers that students present are "gifted" to them by their respected elders. A few numbers are choreographed by the group and their advisor. Dedicated "messengers," the children spend countless hours practicing and perfecting the sign language numbers. It is their goal to speak as one. (Parker 1994, 2)

This formal explanation helped Sue and Wapato Indian Club members situate the sign language routines in terms of connecting to a larger community. The performance of the Lord's Prayer is obviously part of a strong Christian tradition. Although Christianity is not an indigenous Yakama religion, it is a religious tradition that has widespread appeal across the reservation, with many tribal peoples celebrating Christian traditions, often in concert with indigenous traditions.

Ultimately, the Wapato Indian Club framed the sign language performances in terms of helping students learn important lessons of coming

---

[1] In their brochure, the club acknowledges their sign language routines utilize different sign language traditions. Within academic studies, there is a growing attention to American Indian sign languages. For example, see Jeffrey Davis's (2010) excellent work, *Hand Talk*, in which he describes the high detail of lexical similarity between American Sign Language and Plains Indian Sign Language.

WAPATO INDIAN CLUB

Traditional dances and stories of the Yakama Indian Nation

Edited by Lisa Ann Parker

All proceeds benefit the Wapato Indian Club

Figure 1. Wapato Indian Club booklet cover with children signing the Lord's Prayer. (Courtesy of Sue Rigdon)

together as a collective who could "speak as one." The club's booklet states that, historically, sign language helped bridge communication gaps. In contemporary times, doing the sign language routines positioned the children to be proud "messengers" of indigenous peoples—providing Indian and non-Indian audiences the opportunity to see the youth as leaders in the making. The performances were important reminders that leadership, in the Yakama sense, was always tied to the teachings of older generations, as the children learned to lead by sharing a gift bestowed upon them by elders. Additionally, the performance of sign language routines emphasized unity, and the group communicating as a united whole. This emphasis on being committed to the collective is also an important Yakama teaching. Although some status differentials existed within the group (i.e., children with more elaborate regalia would more likely be positioned in front during sign language routines), these statuses were not fixed. For example, if a child with less elaborate regalia was an excellent signer, completing the signs with special grace and precision, then that child would be positioned in a more prominent place for the audience to see. Having elaborate regalia did not always correlate with higher social class standing. Some families had very low socioeconomic standing within mainstream society, yet had wealth in the form of treasured family regalia or had within their family a talented sewer, or bead, quill, or leather worker who could create regalia, often a piece at a time, for the child participating in the Wapato Indian Club. For children whose families did not have regalia and could not afford to sew or bead their own outfits, Wapato Indian Club advisors worked with other parents and community members to sew, loan, and donate outfits, so that no child was turned away for lack of regalia, including non-Indian children. This spirit of generosity and inclusiveness is also a Yakama cultural tradition, with leaders esteemed not because of individual honors or achievement, but because of the ways in which they contribute to the collective good.

Framing their performances in terms that emphasized traditional Yakama cultural values helped ease potential conflict about whether the sign language routines were "authentic" or "genuine," which are common concerns that surround American Indian performances (Wilmer 2009). As such, the sign language performances could be considered an example of "decolonization in unexpected places" as Andrea Smith articulates in her analysis of indigenous people's involvement with Christian evangelism (Smith 2010a).

In reality, the sign language numbers captivated the audiences. Interviewees shared that audiences would often be brought to tears when the children would sign the Lord's Prayer. Theresa Jacob, a Wapato Indian Club parent whose children participated in the club during the 1970s through the 1990s, shared:

> A lot of times people cried during the Lord's Prayer. I think they realized that a culture was being lost and that somehow it was being resurrected, saved. They were Anglos that knew the Lord's Prayer. And to see Indian people in regalia honoring part of their [Anglo]

tradition touched them on an emotional and spiritual level. I mean, they didn't understand the Indian words to the fancy dance songs. Or, the Welcome Dance, they didn't understand those words, but when they played the lady or the man singing the Lord's Prayer, they understood it. [It was in] their own language [English], but they could see the beauty of the sign language. And anybody who was hearing impaired and knew that sign language—that was another culture you were reaching, so I thought it was a win-win. It was always really beautiful.

Theresa's narrative demonstrates the power that cross-cultural communication could have within the Wapato Indian Club performances. In Theresa's interview quote, one can see that the children carried a dual responsibility to represent Indian people and cultures, as well as to reach out to non-Indian audiences who valued a Christian prayer. To do this cross-cultural outreach, Sue taught the children to sign the Lord's Prayer, allowing the children to reach yet another audience in the deaf culture. Outreach to non-Indians was a specific objective of the Wapato Indian Club as Haver Jim, Yakama tribal member and club alumni, who participated in the late 1980s, shared:

I believe that the biggest teaching that I benefited from was exposure to a more contemporary lifestyle, and exposure to the Western culture. You know, the people, they would always talk to you after the performances, or we would go to office gatherings like if Heritage [local college] had a faculty day, we would go perform for them. Or, we'd perform at different businesses in Yakima [a nearby city north of the reservation]. Or, we would go to different events. Thinking back [on my life], I have written down some of the biggest things that had a big influence on me, and my time with the Wapato Indian Club was one of them. And the biggest benefit was being exposed to other cultures. I've been able to be more open, to communicate with the Caucasians or Black people, Mexicans. Sometimes kids [at school] that didn't participate would say, "Oh, quit trying to be an Indian," when they are Indian! I mean, how dumb is that?! It's sad.

Haver credits his participation with the Wapato Indian Club as having a major impact on his adult life. He feels the exposure to non-Indian audiences allowed him to learn to communicate across cultures, and work toward cultural reconciliation. Gaining the strong sense of identity within a supportive environment allowed him to resist negative stereotypes, such as other Native children who teased him for "trying to be Indian" because he showed an interest in learning the routines and performing with the club for non-Native audiences. Haver internalized the positive messages that the club had provided, and as a result he could resist the negative comments about his identity made by some of his peers.

Although he was aware of the value of cross-cultural interactions that the club provided, Haver also reflected on the ways Indian identities could be misunderstood, perhaps even as a result of the performances. He shared:

> The only thing that I think wasn't addressed enough is that powwow is not a religion. You know, powwow performances and all that, dressing up [in regalia], is not spirituality. And I think that was a misconception that a lot of people [non-Indian audiences] had; they viewed that as our form of spirituality. Powwow and performances are completely on their own, contemporary, you know?

Haver's comments distinguish the Wapato Indian Club performances from his spirituality and religion. He views the dance performances, including powwow, as a contemporary pan-Indian cultural expression, which is still important, but does not define his spirituality. He wonders if audiences conflated the two, and hopes that they did not. Yet he realizes that point may have been lost, at times, within the cross-cultural encounters of the Wapato Indian Club performances. However, Haver also acknowledges the importance of engaging non-Indian audiences despite the misunderstanding that might occasionally happen. He recalls that his uncles strongly encouraged him to join the Wapato Indian Club, to help share the club's message that Indians are "still here" and are proud of our cultural traditions. He said:

> We were encouraged to perform, to go show them [our dancing], and it was a matter of fact, to go show them that we're still here. To show them that there are real, real Indians right here, you know, on the reservation! And that was the thing for a long time back then.

Haver outlines important lessons contained within the Wapato Indian Club critical pedagogy. As a dancer, he embodied a proud representation of indigenous people. In doing so, he resisted the stereotype of the "vanished Indian." Haver's leadership within the club helped solidify these critical teachings, and looking back, he understands why his uncles encouraged his participation.

Ryan Craig, a Yakama tribal member and club alumni, participated in the Wapato Indian Club in the 1990s. Ryan is now a DJ with a daily show on the Yakama tribal radio station, KYNR. Ryan is also an accomplished artist, known across Indian country for his musical talent, and has been awarded a prestigious Native American Music award for Hip Hop Artist of the Year. During our interview, Ryan discussed the importance of cultural pride and representation of his people, values he learned in the Wapato Indian Club. He specifically connected his success in the radio and music industries to his participation in the club:

> Just being able to present yourself to non-Indian people and people outside of your own community, even though the job I have now in radio is for the tribal community, it's not just Indians who turn on the radio. It's people of all backgrounds . . . I don't want some rich white people to think that everybody within our tribe is uneducated or everybody within our tribe can't speak on the microphone. So when I would go to those Indian Club trips, we wanted those people to see that Indians aren't stupid. Indians are the ones that are providing the entertainment for them. We didn't have to have their pity or anything like that. So now in my job, when I go on the radio, I don't think of myself like "Oh I'm just at a job for a tribal radio station." No! I want to be better than any radio DJ. Like the Indian Club showed us, just because you're Indian doesn't mean you're less than. Or just because you're not rich, it doesn't mean you can't be somebody in life, because look at all these places you went for all these white people and these rich people doing performances. And that's how I want to live my life now. Being at our tribe's radio station . . . I can be a representation of our entire people, not just myself. I can be the voice of all those classmates and all those people that I grew up with. And then I have the rap thing, making the music and all that, that's pretty much the same as Indian Club, it's just that now it is rap music, we go to shows like at universities. If I was never in Indian Club, I would never know how it feels to be behind that curtain waiting for it to open and go out there.

Ryan's narrative interweaves the lessons he learned as a participant in the Wapato Indian Club with his daily work as a DJ on the tribal radio station and his musical work as a rap artist. The teachings that Indian people must be proud of their identities, resist negative stereotypes, and represent Indian people honorably are lessons that Ryan continues to carry with him on a daily basis. Traveling across the country today to do concerts, Ryan still thinks of his middle-school years standing behind a curtain, dressed in traditional regalia, waiting to perform as part of the Wapato Indian Club dance troupe.

Leadership as Embodied Critical Pedagogy

Revitalizing the traditions of intergenerational teaching and learning helps to fill the cultural knowledge gaps that disrupt indigenous cultural survival. Seeing this gap, and hearing requests from children who were eager to learn the dances, a group of dedicated Yakama people came together to make that education possible. Now, nearly forty years later, the Wapato Indian Club has been teaching children on the Yakama Reservation about traditional dancing and the importance of intergenerational teaching and learning. Contained within those lessons are important teachings about cultural pride, leadership, and responsibility to the future generations. These teachings are the heart of the critical indigenous pedagogy developed within the Wapato Indian Club. Adults involved with the club treated the children with respect so that children could have a safe, fun learning environment. Sue's husband, Mel Rigdon, was another important role model for the children. He remarked that the children called him "grandpa," and indeed, he was a trusted elder who volunteered his time to serve as a chaperone, driver, and sound-system coordinator during performances. In this way, Mel modeled the leadership that Wapato Indian Club advisors hoped to instill in the children. As I examined a collection of archival materials of the Wapato Indian Club (three large boxes of newspaper clippings, programs, and photos held within Sue and Mel Rigdon's home), nearly every photo showed proud Indian children who were representing their people with dignity and respect. As figure 1 shows, the children are embodying the leadership lessons learned within the club.

Archival data included some historical files from the 1950s, in which Yakama families had given family stories to be included in local history projects, an early effort to represent Yakama peoples and perspectives in the curriculum. These took the form of biographies of family members, as well as descriptions of important dances, including the Swan Dance, which is described as an honoring of the swan, whose beauty "has graced our stream and lakes," and with the Yakama women performing the dance, all peoples are reminded that we are blessed in our relationship with mother earth, who provides food and shelter (Rigdon n.d.). From these historical documents, Sue created a curriculum for an Indian cultural class to be offered in the Wapato public schools. The file contains a mimeographed copy of a detailed outline of topics that would be covered in such a class. Attached to the outline is a handwritten note from a school administrator, who states "I'm still not real happy with this outline . . . [it] doesn't really state *how* or with *what* methods the class will be taught—which is the most important factor" and Sue is urged to get in touch with the University of Washington for further guidance (Rigdon n.d.). The administrator's response to the curriculum is indicative of a lack of understanding of indigenous perspectives, histories, and methods for teaching. One of the stated outcomes of the class that Sue had proposed was "being able to state what the idea of Manifest Destiny was and what its significance was in regard to the settlement of the United States." This is a specific outcome that is easily addressed with a critical indigenous perspective of history. A simple method for teaching this is to tell the story of encroachment and land dispossession of Native peoples. Yet, rather than seeing the value and potential of this form of critical education, the administrator questions the curriculum. This political context encouraged such teachings to take place in an extracurricular capacity, rather than during the regular academic periods of the school day. This decision had strategic implications. As a club, rather than a class, the Wapato Indian Club could have the freedom to bring in elders to teach via oral histories, role modeling, and with song, all of which are indigenous pedagogies that sometimes face scrutiny in Western educational systems, due to confusion about curriculum rigor, assessment, relevance, and importance.

Once established as a club, the critical pedagogy of the Wapato Indian Club focused on preparing the next generation to be strong leaders. This point was touched on across all interviews that I conducted. For example, Ryan reflected on the importance of reaching out and providing encouragement. In his comments, he spoke about the challenges of sustaining cultural revitalization efforts, like the Wapato Indian Club, and how future leaders may feel it is difficult to fill the shoes of our beloved elders:

> After Sue [founding Wapato Indian Club advisor] retired, it would be hard to pick it up where she left off. She had it to where Wapato Indian Club was like professionals. And everybody knew that. And that is why she got all the recognition that she did, and she deserved that recognition, but, I guess we just need a few leaders to step up

and then be the ones that influence people. For example, for me at the radio station, let's say if I never went into radio, you wouldn't have anybody there under the age of fifty years old. Ok? And if I were in some other field, I would never want to be a part of it. But if I'm twenty-eight, and I'm able to influence people that are twenty-one, and fourteen, and even as young as five and six years old, then that's a start, and that's where we're going to build it from.

Now with Wapato Indian Club, you have Adam [a current Wapato Indian Club advisor]. Adam's a basketball coach, and he's a really good guy. If he can influence those students to say, "Hey, you should come be a part of this Indian Club," "Maybe we can set up these performances," or "Maybe we can do this and do that." If he can get those one or two kids to step up and be leaders and decide they want to have kids take pride in their culture and heritage and our tribe, that's the first step. Because the reality is that it was Sue that got people to be a part of it. If nobody would have said [to me] "Hey, you should come sign up for this," or, "You should come on these trips," I wouldn't have gone, because I was a kid; I didn't know. But if Adam can be that one to take that one leader who is maybe a seventh or eighth grader and if that one leader can be a positive role model for the sixth graders, and those sixth graders can be role models for their younger siblings, it will be right there. That's the point.

The point is that I can live my life and I can be mad about this happening to me, or "I don't have this," or, "I don't get paid enough for that," or, "All my classmates or some of my relatives are on drugs or alcohol." I can sit around and I can pout, and I can be mad that our tribe doesn't do this, or our tribe doesn't do that. Or, I could go live my life and do the best that I can in everything I'm involved in. And then somebody's going to look at me and say, "Hey he's still doing his best and he's still doing what he loves to do." And if that person does that, then it is like a domino effect.

In his interview, Ryan reflects on the rich meaning that his participation in the Wapato Indian Club held for him. He continues to carry those teachings with him, and he has a vision of leadership and social change that is rooted in the lessons that he learned in the club. He articulates that it takes a caring elder to reach out and teach the younger generations, to encourage and inspire the young people to reach their potential and to emerge as a leader in whatever field they pursue. Ryan also mentions that Sue's leadership earned her numerous awards. For example, Sue was honored for her work with the Wapato Indian Club when she was named Woman of the Year in 1999 at a gala event hosted by the Larson Gallery and the Yakima Valley Community College Women's Program (Cooper 1999). Ryan respects Sue's strong leadership and example, and he internalized the positive role modeling she provided. In this way, the powerful messages of the Wapato Indian Club dance troupe continue to transcend space and time, leaving a positive legacy on the reservation and beyond.

Critical Pedagogy as a Tool to Heal the Soul Wounds of Colonialism

Haver discussed the ways that participating in the Wapato Indian Club influenced him. He recalled that one of the most powerful experiences was helping to teach younger students how to dance. Beyond teaching them a series of steps and movements, Haver helped mentor them on how to carry themselves as proud and healthy Yakama people who were free of bitterness and hatred. He said:

> And so participating in something like that was a way to bring those children in. You know, to teach them, but to teach them in a good way. That was the hard part, because I have so much anger, or hatred or bitterness towards the white race because of the stories that I heard.

Haver goes on to clarify that during his childhood he heard the oral histories of genocide and colonization inflicted upon Indian peoples. These teachings sometimes stirred ill feelings toward non-Indians, who were the primary audiences for Wapato Indian Club performances. At times he struggled to overcome feelings of negativity, because of, he said,

> the things I was taught. But at the same exact time I was taught that, not to hate them [whites], because it's not directly their fault. 'Cause the people that did that died a long time ago. But to know that they still carry that same trait. I don't know if you call it genetic trait or whatever it is that they carry inside them, they brought from Europe, that was what I was told. Maybe this generation won't be that way. But our job as performers was to try to maintain that understanding of peace. You know it was hard to understand that as a child. And those are the things that I've reflected on.

In his narrative, Haver describes how his participation in the Wapato Indian Club helped him process the seeming contradictory teachings that he learned at home—about remembering the violent past and genocide of our people but moving forward in a peaceful way. As a child, it was difficult for him to understand the expectations placed on him by his elders, who shared these teachings with him. Within the Wapato Indian Club, when Haver became a lead male dancer, he was responsible for teaching and mentoring younger students. He had to decide which teachings he would focus on in his work with the other students. Haver looked to Sue, the advisor of the club, for guidance, and he articulates in his interview that it was clear to him that his responsibility as a Wapato Indian Club performer was to maintain that understanding of peace across cultures and races.

This teaching of peace was important to Sue and other adults involved with the Wapato Indian Club because of the violent social and historical context in which the children were living. The club was founded amid unprecedented crime and violence in Wapato and within the school. Local news files at the Yakima Valley Regional Library contain headlines of Wapato's gang and drug violence problems in the 1970s and early 1980s. But then, a shift in discourse takes place, as culturally focused youth activities begin taking hold within the school, with Sue Rigdon involved in many of these efforts. One example was the Cultural Unity Fair, a celebration of food, dance, and culture that involved all students, teachers, and staff at the Wapato Middle School. Within the news file, a noticeable shift takes place. Eventually, the Wapato headlines begin to be dominated by the children who are embracing their cultures and sharing them with the community and other audiences. The headlines of drugs and gang warfare begin to fade into the background.

While we cannot draw a simple causal arrow between youth cultural activities and the reduction of gang and drug crimes, we also cannot deny any connection. Haver talked about the connection that he saw between these phenomena. In his interview, he spoke generally about the difficulties facing Indian people in and around the Yakama Reservation. He remembered how, during his youth, drugs and gangs were prevalent; they

> swept up so many people, hundreds of people. You know at that time I didn't understand why it was such an urgency, and I think that is what contributed to the popularity of Wapato Indian Club. Back then [the club] used to be in the newspaper; it was a big thing. Because, and I think that is why it was such a big thing, because there

were just so many people dying, the death rate was so high, that it [the club] was the one good thing that was coming out of our community, you know? And I think that is why it was such a big thing. And you know, there's such a large, that large number of people that had died at that time . . . It took me my whole life to understand this stuff.

During his interview, Haver recalls his middle-school days and the overwhelming grief and suffering he witnessed within the community due to the violence and death attributed to gangs and drugs. He specifically remembers the numerous funerals he attended, and how it was difficult for him to make sense of it all as a child. US Department of Justice statistics confirm Haver's memories of violence in Indian Country. In a decade-long study (1992–2002), the Department of Justice reports that American Indians experienced a per capita rate of violence twice that of the US population (United States Department of Justice Office of Justice Programs 2004). Perhaps even more disturbing is that "American Indians experienced an estimated 1 violent crime for every 10 residents age 12 or older" (United States Department of Justice Office of Justice Programs 2004, iv). While the Wapato Indian Club helped protect Haver from some of the violence around him as a middle-school student, eventually he, too, had struggles with substance abuse. He shared:

You know I battled, seriously battled with alcoholism and drug use myself. To the point where I was in the hospital, going to admit myself to the psych ward, and if it wasn't for a picture of my auntie on the wall, I was walking down the hallway and I saw her picture there and she was in her outfit just like that, but she had a hat on [he is pointing to a portrait of a person wearing their traditional regalia]. And she is the one who gave me my Indian name, you know. And right next to her was another picture a little bigger than that one of two sweathouses and this was five years ago in Seattle Harborview Medical Center and I tried to overdose 'cause I had that pain that I speak of was so overwhelming that you know I didn't know of any other way but suicide, because you know, you see it so *much* your whole life . . . when I was in treatment they tried to diagnose me and give me medication and I told them no, I know what is wrong with me. Just leave me alone, all I need is to get away from everybody. You know, get back to myself. And so yeah, and all the scars on my body are a testament to the battles that I've been through. You know physical contact with my environment. And people in my environment. And that's what I want to do with my own work, in school, my research. You know, to learn how to, with sociolinguistics, to be able to develop programs in language and things like the Wapato Indian Club. So I think it is, in the sense of all the things that our people have been through, where we're at now is a very large leap into that healing process. A gigantic leap.

Haver goes on to further credit Sue's tireless efforts to help the children. He refers to her work as the foundation of all the good work that club alumni will do in the future. In an analysis of his comments, the activism of club alumni is apparent as part of an intergenerational effort to heal our people:

> You know, I think that Sue's dedication is, how would you say, a very strong placing stone, I guess you could say. You know, something that, in history, is there. She held us there just long enough. And I think with the support of the community, with the families that participated, maybe they couldn't get as far as we could, but just because they were there now, we can get a little bit farther.

Haver recalls the crucial support that Sue provided during his youth. The Wapato Indian Club gave him an opportunity to begin healing; it uniquely connected him with his own culture and with other cultures. He uses the memories and examples of the Wapato Indian Club to inform his own scholarship and work. As a reentry student at Heritage University, a local university, Haver is inspired to use his studies to develop youth programs similar to the Wapato Indian Club and to continue helping nurture the next generation of leaders on Yakama homeland.

Core Values and the Wapato Indian Club's Model of Indigenous Social Change

From its inception, the Wapato Indian Club has advanced what indigenous studies scholars would call a decolonizing agenda. Indigenous youth, resisting an assimilationist agenda of the settler-colonial education system, insisted that their cultures and traditional teachings be offered to them. By analyzing the critical pedagogical work and politics of the Wapato Indian

Club, we can understand the important place of indigenous youth and their allies in cultural revitalization efforts.

After analyzing interview data and the limited archival material about Wapato Indian Club, I created a list of core values that served as the foundation of all the work done in the club. In my second interview with Sue, I shared the list with her, and we talked about each value, and any possible revisions that the list might need. Ultimately, we finalized the following list: Respect, Inclusivity, Responsibility, Self-Awareness, Listening, Healing, and Unity.

These are the core values that guide the club. They are the basis of how the club teaches youth "how to be" in accordance with elders' instructions. Even decades later, alumni are able to articulate how their participation in Wapato Indian Club helps them to continue striving for these ideals, as Haver articulates so eloquently. By carefully listening to participants' narratives, I was able to envision a model that would represent the Wapato Indian Club and the process of teaching the core values to participants. But I knew that this model needed to be something more than an assemblage of arrows and boxes. I wanted the model to be rooted in the culturally based stories and teachings that were so precious to the people involved in the Wapato Indian Club. Below, in figure 2, I share my conceptualization of this emerging model. Within the model, there are representations of powerful features of the bird who was so important in the Wapato Indian Club performances—the swan, *wawḵilúuk*, who is sacred to Plateau peoples. It is a being that is strong and enduring, and is a powerful place-based example for our people. Its elegance reminds us of the beauty of our traditions, and its graceful flight provides a guiding light that the club follows, always striving and reaching toward a gracefulness and discipline that will bring about healing and unity. As the archival materials and interview data quoted within this chapter indicate, the swan was an important symbol to communicate the message of respecting all creation and paying honor to nature through performances. Within the model, the swan itself embodies the core values taught within the Wapato Indian Club, serving as a reflection of and an image of guidance for the critical pedagogy used within the club. As the swan embodies the teachings, so too are the children expected to embody these values, as they learn and carry on the teachings of their elders. As such, the children's bodies become a site for critical pedagogy. The praxis developed in the Wapato Indian Club thus contributes to our understanding of indigenous social change theories, encouraging us to remember the potential and

Figure 2. Wapato Indian Club model. (Drawing by Michelle M. Jacob and Christopher J. Andersen)

contribution of recognizing young people's leadership and the importance of the body as a liberatory tool for critical awareness, leadership development, and decolonizing praxis.

This model provides an example of a decolonizing praxis that emphasizes the importance of the local context and the connection to place-based teachings. It encourages all peoples to build a relationship with the special beings/relatives with whom they share the land. According to indigenous teachings, the Creator has placed important teachers, like the swan, in our presence, and we have the honor to learn from these beings/relatives. The model I provide here demonstrates the importance of an indigenous place-based paradigm for learning and teaching.

CHAPTER TWO

I Don't Want Our Language to Die

Indigenous Language Revitalization, Survivance, and the Stakes of Building a Moral Community

An Ethnographic Introduction: Dancing to Honor the Past, Present, and Future

*   *   *

We sit around a table at the university cafeteria, enjoying our lunch together. Then, all of a sudden, the elder announces that she would like to have dancers at the honor dinner tomorrow night. Word quickly spreads across the lunchroom. Soon a practice session is organized, and several women have committed to dancing. The elder is pleased and agrees to help teach the dance during the practice session.

Later that afternoon, the women assemble in the longhouse on campus. The elder scans the room until she finds suitable instruments. She uses a spatula and a cardboard box as a makeshift hand drum. Upon testing out her new "drum," she explains the legend that accompanies the song she will be singing, and she reminds the women of the dance steps for the Farewell Dance. The legend that she shares is place-based, reminding us of our surroundings and the legendary beings who shaped the world before our time, from the ocean to the Columbia River Gorge to places in between. This particular legend explains the formation of Beacon Rock, a prominent landmark that stands next to the Columbia River.

As elders do, she explains how she learned the song and dance. She tells a story of when she was a young girl, perhaps fourteen years old, when she and her friends were asked to do the Farewell Dance at the longhouse. The young women were selected to do the honor of bidding the guests a safe journey home. The elder remembers the occasion fondly, and through her storytelling, she connects generations of storytellers, singers, dancers, and guests.

After this storytelling, the elder reminds the women that they need to practice. The women line up and begin the dance. Several rounds later, the women agree that they feel ready to dance at the important dinner tomorrow night. At the dinner, two men will be honored for their support of the Northwest Indian Language Institute and the summer program designed to help train tribal language teachers. The elder's singing and storytelling, and the women's dancing, will be special offerings of thanksgiving for all of the support that the entire community has provided.

*   *   *

Settler-Colonial Violence and Language Loss

This chapter addresses contemporary language revitalization efforts on the Yakama Reservation and focuses on the activism involved in building a partnership with the Northwest Indian Language Institute at the University of Oregon. The activists' work is a response to a realization that language loss is one of the most important contemporary issues facing indigenous communities today (Meek 2010; Silver and Miller 1997). I draw from interviews with seven people involved with the partnership to analyze how their efforts validate the importance of indigenous survivance, build a moral community, and contribute to our understanding of indigenous decolonization efforts.

A century after the Yakama Treaty of 1855 was signed, Yakama peoples continued to grapple with social, political, and economic forces that brought sweeping changes. In the 1950s, many Yakama families continued to participate in our people's traditional economic activities, including seasonal rounds of hunting, gathering, and fishing. However, these traditional activities were, more and more, being juggled along with efforts to be "modern." This ability to merge traditional and contemporary economic practices was a phenomenon that took place across Northwest tribes (Raibmon 2005). Working in the canneries and agricultural fields, and sending children to the White man's school, became a larger part of the typical Yakama family's life. These social changes had implications for our community's "language ideologies," which Field and Kroskrity define as "beliefs and feelings about language . . . language shift and language death" (Field and Kroskrity 2009, 4).

Ultimately, we can trace the roots of our language loss back to a history of policy-making designed to destroy Native languages, cultures, and peoples, in a process that Teresa McCarty refers to as "social architecture" (McCarty 2011). In the federal policy era of "termination" and with the continual assault upon indigenous people's lives and rights, Yakama people made difficult decisions about how to raise their children, including whether and where they should attend school, and which language or languages should be spoken at home. Interviewees shared family stories about how this era was a time when elders and parents began refusing to speak our language to children, thinking that it was better for the younger generation to learn the "White man's" ways, with the hopes that they would escape some of the brutal hostility, discrimination, and violence that was widespread in Indians' lives, both on and off the reservation.

These examples of political and social injustices help illustrate the many social forces that are at work in Yakama peoples' lives. Sometimes it is a difficult question for outsiders to understand: "Why are indigenous languages dying?" The answer lies tangled within the social context and struggles that represent indigenous peoples' efforts to maintain their traditional land bases and cultures. As Field and Kroskrity acknowledge, "Language ideologies are thus grounded in the social distribution of both indigenous social inequality and the differential impact of colonial and postcolonial contact experiences" (6). These difficult decisions provide important context for understanding how government policies (energy, education, economic) are far from simply detached bureaucratic decisions. Rather, policies have a deep impact on Native communities, at times shaking the social order at its very foundation. As McCarty articulates, "[p]olicy is not a disembodied thing, but rather a situated sociocultural process—the complex of practices, ideologies, attitudes, and formal and informal mechanisms that influence people's language choices in profound and pervasive everyday ways" (McCarty 2011, xii). Thus, state- and federal-level educational policymakers who privilege English-only and English-dominant educational policies are actually contributing to a "form of linguistic and/or cultural genocide" among indigenous peoples (Skutnabb-Kangas and Dunbar 2010, 12).

Activists involved with the Yakama-NILI partnership recognize the importance of Yakama views helping to shape policy. One interviewee, Patsy Whitefoot, is a Yakama tribal member who works for the Toppenish

School District on the Yakama Reservation. She also helps coordinate several drug and alcohol prevention initiatives for youth on the reservation. Patsy is a nationally recognized leader in Indian education efforts, serving as the past president of the National Indian Education Association and the Washington Indian Education Association. She has been involved with the Yakama-NILI partnership, and in her interview, she mentioned the importance of language, identity, and history. Her words remind us of the stakes of language revitalization:

> We all are working toward the common goal of raising healthy children, and working toward community wellness is what I think makes a big difference in trying to maintain who we are in terms of sovereignty and our treaty, but also in terms of our language, and our tradition and our culture . . . helping our children to be able to identify with their heritage and who they are.

Patsy reminds us that one of the major stakes of decolonizing work is to protect the identities of indigenous youth. She links our people's collective well-being ("community wellness" and "sovereignty" in her words) with children's ability to have healthy indigenous identities. In her work with young people, Patsy sees how they struggle to build healthy identities. Young people too often suffer with substance abuse, self-harm, and a lack of self-esteem. Yet Patsy also knows that being strongly rooted in one's indigenous culture (language, tradition, and culture—as she states) helps serve as a protective factor for youth. Thus, language revitalization work is inherently decolonizing, as it allows greater access to language knowledge and use for future generations, and provides the opportunity for young indigenous people to develop healthy identities.

Indigenous Resistance and Its Complications: Language Survivance

Several interviewees spoke about the direct link between government policies of assimilation and our people's language loss, a result of settler colonialism that activists are mindfully working to resist. Greg Sutterlict, a Yakama tribal member who has dedicated his life to preserving and revitalizing our tribe's language, spoke to this point as he recounted the historical narrative of language loss within his own family. Greg began his grassroots language revitalization work when he was a young adult, and has spent nearly twenty years working closely with and learning from our revered elder and master speaker, Dr. Virginia Beavert, Tuẋámshish.

In Greg's narrative, there is an implicit reference to what Eduardo Duran and Bonnie Duran have noted as the "soul wound" of colonialism, resulting from intergenerational historical trauma (Duran 2006; Duran and Duran 1995). If that wound is not healed, then it will persist and worsen across generations. I examine social problems in terms of language loss being evidence of a soul wound, with language revitalization efforts as an expression of healing those wounds. For example, in Greg's interview he discussed the language knowledge gap within his own family, which is tied to the legacy of historical trauma and the Indian boarding schools. Greg's father attended Indian boarding school, where he was taught that Indian traditions were evil. His father internalized these teachings and hesitated to engage in cultural traditions, including speaking the language. As a result, Greg only learned a limited Ichishkíin vocabulary as a youth. When he was a teenager, Greg talked with his great-grandfather about the language. His great-grandfather, an Ichishkíin speaker, explained to Greg, "You know, they really tortured us at the boarding schools for speaking the language, and that's why I never wanted you to learn. Now I wish I would have taught you, but it's too late."

The words of his elder stuck with Greg. He grew up being aware of the damage and trauma that the boarding schools had inflicted upon his family. Then, as a young adult, he had the opportunity to begin taking language classes from Virginia Beavert, our tribal elder who had written the first practical dictionary of our language, and completed the first comprehensive dictionary of Ichishkíin in collaboration with Sharon Hargus at the University of Washington (Beavert and Hargus 2009). In recognition of all of her work with the language, Virginia was awarded an honorary doctorate degree from the University of Washington. Additionally, she earned her PhD in linguistics at the University of Oregon at the age of ninety. When Virginia offered introductory Ichishkíin classes at Heritage University on the Yakama Reservation, Greg and his friends, Roger and Rose, whom I will quote later, found themselves in her classes together in the 1990s. They continue to study with Virginia, extending their learning time outside of the classroom and into their homes, together in the mountains, at community events, and at ceremonial gatherings. Virginia and her students have worked, over the years, to brainstorm, develop, and revise curriculum, attain formal education, and engage in significant community outreach. They have collaborated to create tapes and CDs of language lessons and recordings to distribute within the community. In these ways, this small core of activists has helped to subvert the colonial assimilationist agenda designed to eliminate our language. Their work to recover, reclaim, and revitalize our language is a powerful form of resistance to the ongoing effects of colonialism.

Intergenerational Responsibility and Indigenous Resistance

Indigenous resistance movements place a strong emphasis on intergenerational responsibility. Indigenous scholar Taiaiake Alfred discusses this phenomenon in his study of indigenous activists and leaders, who told him, "Our youth always need people to look up to, because if you don't have people to look up to, you don't have any idea about where you want to go with your life. If you see a strong role model in front of you, it leads you in a good direction. You always need people to make pathways for you to follow" (Alfred 2005, 260).

Indigenous resistance is inherently intergenerational. Without the guidance of elders, younger generations will not have a pathway to follow. These intergenerational connections are important for all aspects of culture, and especially so for language, due to the predominance of the English language among American Indian children, families, schools, and the broader US society. Some indigenous language scholars have identified the US educational policy of "English only" as a form of subtractive education that harms all peoples and results in ethnocide, linguistic genocide, and ultimately, a crime against humanity (Skutnabb-Kangas and Dunbar 2010). Part of this destruction is due to the devaluing of elders in contemporary indigenous societies. Jeffrey Anderson writes about the implications of elders losing their high status, noting the "elders were once the center of all ideological production, including ideologies about language, culture, and religion" (Anderson 2009, 58). Thus, contemporary efforts to revitalize our language represent an important form of indigenous resistance.

Resisting the effects of colonialism is nothing new for Yakama peoples. In the introduction to this book, I provided several historical examples of Yakama peoples who dared to challenge the system, holding the US government accountable for violating our people's rights and lands, and for threatening our cultural well-being. Yet efforts to resist the ongoing effects of colonialism continue to be undermined by the overall lack of resources within Indian country. Grassroots activists acknowledge this dilemma, noting that relying on federal funds, or the leadership of the tribal government, are not, in and of themselves, sufficient answers to our peoples' language loss problem. Thus, there is a strong need and important role for grassroots activism in the struggle to protect and revitalize indigenous languages. A reliance on governmental institutions will not solve our problems for us.

There are varying reasons why tribal and non-tribal governmental institutions, whether political or educational, fail to serve Indian peoples' needs. As George Castile points out in his critical analysis of the history of Indian self-determination, "So long as tribal governments must rely on the federal government for the vast majority of their funding, there must inevitably continue a pattern of federal oversight, hence some degree of 'paternalism'" (Castile 2006, 117). Castile states that self-determination, within a contemporary context, really means self-*administration* of federally funded programs. Such an approach is clearly limited, with significant resources spent simply trying to follow or demonstrate "compliance" with bureaucratic governmental regulations, rather than addressing community needs from an indigenous perspective. Other scholars have noted that tribal governments are simply overwhelmed, or stretched too thin, by "functional overload," as community members expect timely solutions from a tribal government structure with limited resources and heavy demands (Cornell 2007). Again, the overall lack of resources, along with the tedious oversight and regulations attached to the limited federal funding available, creates a sociopolitical context in which the hard work of language preservation and revitalization is often marginalized.

Noting the scarcity of resources on the reservation, and the limited leadership and support from both tribal and local educational institutions, grassroots activists created a strategy to work with "whomever wanted to help" and "had a good heart to help." This meant working largely outside of the tribal government structure. The lack of material resources available on the reservation led language activists to partner with educational institutions and linguists who *did* engage in culturally appropriate, sensitive, and enthusiastic outreach with tribal peoples. For example, Sharon Hargus, Janne Underriner, Joana Jansen, Scott Delancy, and Bruce Rigsby were mentioned as academic linguists who were committed to supporting indigenous communities' language revitalization. These academics are part of a larger network of linguists who have helped to shed light on the importance of indigenous language preservation and revitalization, with several examples of scholarship and nonprofit work that supports community language work.[1] Some of this work was funded by the National Science Foundation or the Administration for Native Americans, but oftentimes activists have paid for their travel, tuition, and other costs out of their own pockets. Sometimes the most supportive institutions were over a thousand miles away, which meant that tribal peoples had to leave their families, homes, and jobs to pursue the opportunity to learn about language revitalization issues and methods that could serve their home communities. For example, Roger Jacob Jr. credits the University of Arizona American Indian Language Development Institute (AILDI), and the fellowship he received to attend the institute, for helping him understand the urgency of protecting and revitalizing the language:

I'm down there [with Virginia], we were down there as a pair . . . I think there were ten pairs. There were twenty of us. And we were representing the Yakamas. You know, it was competitive and they made us really feel like it was an honor to be selected. And it was down there that I learned that our, that Ichishkíin, our Yakama language, was endangered, more so than salmon or steelhead or spotted owls. There are fewer Ichishkíin speakers, or Yakama speakers here on our reservation than spotted owls, and we're a timber tribe. At the time I had a master's degree in resource management and worked for the Yakama Nation in resource management, and so I was able to make that connection and that is the first time, I'd been studying the language for years, and would just kind of do my thing, and the light came on, and it was, "Holy moly!" This thing is endangered and it is important, just how biological diversity is something you know, that is good, and you know, we should be trying to protect, we need to be doing the same thing for these languages, and then this language that I was studying, and could read and write and was getting better at speaking all the time, was one of those. It was worse than spotted owls, and salmon, and the steelhead. It was really eye opening for me.

Roger's experience at AILDI helped him make a connection between his natural resources management background and his work with Ichishkíin. Drawing from an environmental protection framework of needing to

---

[1]For example, see Barbra Meek's (2010) book. Another example is the Advocates for Indigenous California Language Survival, which builds upon Leanne Hinton's renowned work in master-apprentice language learning (Advocates for Indigenous California Language Survival 2012).

"protect endangered resources," Roger recognized the intense political and economic mobilization that occurred to save precious natural resources (birds and fish). He connected this mobilization of resources to "protect what is important" to the survival of his indigenous language. In doing so, Roger began to realize how crucial his work with the language was, so that he could serve as an advocate to help ensure the language survived. Roger's analysis of the need to mobilize resources to protect what is valuable resonates with contemporary indigenous human rights discourse. In chapter 4, I discuss the stakes of cultural revitalization in terms of access to culture and language as a right. Roger's narrative helps tie together the important perspectives of language conceptualized as a both a *right* (that should survive for future generations), and as a *resource* (to be drawn on because of the unique cultural and scientific knowledge embedded in the language) (McCarty 2011). Roger, and his tribal people, benefited from the University of Arizona's outreach to him, and the applied linguistics framework that Roger learned helped further spark his interest and cemented his commitment to continuing to work toward revitalizing the language.

Virginia also noted the importance of universities doing partnership work with tribal peoples to support language revitalization. In her interview, she discussed the significant outreach of the University of Oregon Northwest Indian Language Institute (NILI), and explained how it led to a long-term partnership in which both the university and tribal peoples benefited through language revitalization efforts that were dedicated to practical and applied work:

MJ: So how did you get started working with NILI?

VIRGINIA: Janne Underriner [NILI Director] sent me a letter and she wanted to know if I would volunteer to help out in developing something for Indian education over there [at the University of Oregon] on the culture level. She needed a resource person. And so I told her that I would gladly do it. So I went over there. Whenever they had a meeting the Warm Springs and the Umatilla came, and each tribe, and the Nespeelam Indians and the Grand Ronde. They didn't have anyone from Yakama except me. So I sat in the meetings and helped out. And I became more interested in what they were doing. The people that were involved were so enthusiastic about developing materials for the tribes that it was commendable. Because those tribes now are using those materials. And the training that they gave them during the summer, you know the teachers, they invite the teachers to come in and do you know, they have workshops to attend, how to develop their training as teachers, how to develop their own curriculum, and how to teach it. And all of those things, you know, that the teacher would need. So this is very important. And I'm glad that I started, and this was way back, in 1998, too . . . it really makes me feel glad to see so many Yakamas coming now to the workshop . . . And we're training other people to become more professional over there. And we've enticed two young men to come to the university to actually get their professional degree. And one has graduated. And I have one more left, and I have two girls, apprentices over there, they're not Yakamas, but they're going to be linguists and they're going to go out to the reservation and help out, whichever tribe is interested in them later on. And so that is how I'm working. I'm too old now to actually go out and do any fieldwork, so what I do is just kind of stay put and have everyone come to me, you know. I'm not much into technology anymore. So I just let the young people do the technology work. And I provide the language and knowledge about my culture, but I don't want anyone to believe that I know everything. I only know what I learned in my childhood through my grandmother, great-grandmother, and my mother, and my father. My father was a full-blood Indian who never went to school, and so was my mother. My mother never went to school either, but they were raised in the old way.

Virginia's narrative shares that her involvement building a partnership with NILI has focused on fulfilling practical needs within tribal communities (training people how to teach the language) and accessing the resources of the university to benefit tribal communities (degree programs that produce linguists who can serve tribal communities), and combines traditional forms of knowledge with the technologies of the university (humbly drawing from the teachings that her elders provided to help students who are learning language structure and documentation). Virginia is a renowned tribal elder and a master speaker of Sahaptin, yet she also brings an attitude of humility to her work. In her narrative she refuses to be called an "expert" and insists that all she knows is what her traditional elders taught her. Virginia's expertise, however, is invaluable to Ichishkíin learners, who need the cultural teachings to fully understand and grasp the intricacies of the language. Many Yakama elders who hold the traditional teachings have passed on, which, along with dramatic social changes, has left a cultural knowledge gap.

In his interview, Roger spoke of the social change and the resulting decline of language use that he has witnessed over the past forty years. He discussed the stakes of such changes in practical, applied, and spiritual terms. I asked him what language loss means to a community. He responded:

> Language is the *foundation* of culture, and without the language, what kind of tribe are you? Without the language, all the priorities, all the things that made you that tribe, your ancestors, all the things that you ate, places that you went, the foods you gathered, materials you gathered, the medicines, all of that, that can really only be truly expressed in the language and that's what makes you unique as a tribe. Otherwise, things are getting pan-Indian or just all washed out, and being American. That's really where the rubber hits the road in terms of trying to hold on to your true tribal identity, I mean, I think could only express it in the language. What are your priority foods? Why are you still here today? How did your people stay alive? When they got sick or when somebody was going to give birth, how did they carry these things out? Or burials, ceremonies, name givings, trading, weddings, the things that were prioritized and used and the terminology and all that, it's expressed in the language.

In his response, Roger questions whether a tribal community could meaningfully exist without the language, noting the many forms of knowledge contained with the language. He links this cultural knowledge to the survival of the people. Within Roger's narrative is an emphasis on the value of applied knowledge. His words urge readers to think about practical questions, to remember the traditions and seek out the knowledge and teachings of the older generations, so tribal peoples can confidently answer questions like "What did our ancestors use to survive?" Such teachings are important to Roger because of his understanding that the current generations would simply not be here without the knowledge, wisdom, and teachings of the past generations. Roger's analysis of the importance of language and culture is an expression of what Gerald Vizenor (2008) has termed "survivance." Vizenor defines survivance as "the action, condition, quality, and sentiments of the verb 'survive, to remain alive or in existence,' to outlive, persevere with a suffix of survivancy" (19). The examples Roger discusses help us understand the breadth and depth of the meaning of cultural survivance within contemporary indigenous communities. His narrative reminds us of the stakes of cultural revitalization work: individual cultural identity, collective tribal identity, and rites of passage and ceremonies that teach us how to survive as Yakama people—these important lessons are all contained within the language. Thus, the survival of Ichishkíin is necessary for the survival of Yakama culture and people.

While such narratives emphasize the practical and applied vision of education, Roger also elaborated on the spiritual significance and importance of cultural revitalization education. He stated:

> Once you start doing ceremonies in English, I mean even like a salmon. We're considered a salmon tribe. Sometimes when you go to a feast in the longhouse, and show respect for that fish that is responsible for us being here to this day, how many people even understand that? We respect that, and we have a ceremony and give it heightened importance. In English you would try to say we recognize it as a communion food and we have a special name for it, like the everyday name for salmon would be *nusux̱*, and then when you take it into your body and really show it respect and give thanks for it, and recognize how important it is and take it in as a first food at the *káatnam* (longhouse) and you would refer to it or hear it referred to as *Waykáanash* (sacred name for Chinook salmon). And it's not done all the time, and people are forgetting that. Pretty soon it will just be something in a can that you buy at the store. Pretty soon it won't even be that. They'll just be eating McDonald's, or white bread and bologna. What kind of tribe is that?

Roger links language survival with the survival of our tribal peoples, as the knowledge systems contained within Ichishkíin are important from a natural resources perspective, a nutritional perspective, and a spiritual perspective. When language use and practice are diminished, the spiritual power and abilities of our people are likewise diminished, raising questions about identity, culture, and language practice. Roger's concerns with survivance are similar to the questions raised in Sheilah Nicholas's study of Hopi language practice, when one of her tribal elders asked, "How are you Hopi if you can't speak it?" (Nicholas 2011, 53). The very survival of the people depends on the survival of the language. This worries Roger, but his work to revitalize the language is a powerful example of healing both on the individual level as well as on the community level. He shared that his work with the language taught him many things, but most of all, how to "be a better person." Ultimately, the struggle in which indigenous peoples engage to protect our bodies, lands, foods, and traditions is about helping us to live up to our fullest potential as indigenous peoples. Roger's narrative helps teach us that indigenous languages hold within them the culturally based teachings for accomplishing this.

Rose Mary Miller also viewed language revitalization as crucial for our people's survival and well-being. In her interview, Rose shared that she started learning the language as an adult. Her work with the language was inspired by her own settler-colonial–imposed knowledge gap, which she linked to the boarding schools:

> I didn't start language classes again with Virginia until the early 1990s . . . I always wanted to learn my language. Mom chose not to teach us the language. She went to the boarding school and didn't want to do that.

Rose's family was wounded by the boarding school experience. Because of the messages that her mother had internalized from the government boarding school experience, her mother did not teach Rose the traditional teachings or use the language within their home. Rose's mom had done so because of a belief that her daughter could not be "successful" within US society if they spoke their Native language. Rose's mother was trying to protect her daughter from the harsh treatment she witnessed at the boarding school. As a result, the assimilationist agenda of "detribalizing" Indian children is enforced, which was the top priority of the Indian boarding schools (Lomawaima 1994). Yet Rose did not accept that assimilation was the only option. Rose felt called to learn the teachings and to embrace her Native identity. She turned to other family members who helped her learn some of the traditions. She shared: "I always wanted to identify with my Native culture. I started hanging out with my cousins." This strong sense of identity is what led Rose to Virginia's language classes as an adult. Now, over twenty years later, Rose is an active member of the decolonizing movement to revitalize the language, serving as a language teacher within the public school system on the reservation. She is helping to fill the knowledge gaps of the younger generations. Her presence and her classes help to decolonize the settler-colonial education system for the next generation. Rose considers her work with the students to be part of the language revitalization activist movement because she connects our people's survival with the knowledge and use of Ichishkíin. She discussed this point in terms of our treaty:

A lot of our treaty is based on our culture. If we lose that, the government can abrogate our treaty. Our people can't survive without the treaty. We'd lose our land base. Too many terrible things would happen. I've always wanted to push the language.

Rose engages in language revitalization as part of a broader vision to protect our people. She views our peoples' rights and healthy survival as *dependent* upon our knowledge and use of Ichishkíin. Carrying on the teaching and learning of Ichishkíin, then, is central to indigenous survivance. Rose clearly articulates that our people will be weakened without the language, our culture, and treaty rights. The primary way that Rose engages in cultural survivance work is through her teaching language classes. Rose teaches within the K–12 public school system and at community classes within the housing projects on the reservation. Rose credits Virginia and NILI with her growth as a teacher over the years. Virginia "insisted" that Rose attend the NILI Summer Institute, according to Rose. At NILI, Rose learned teaching methods and applied linguistics that have helped her excel as a language teacher, earning her an Educator of the Year award (Washington State Indian Education Association 2012). Rose continues to attend the NILI Summer Institute, and she sees her skills growing each year. Teaching is inspiring and fulfilling for Rose. She views language learning as important for everyone, articulating an inclusive vision of decolonizing work. Rose shared:

> We are interested in teaching people at all levels. We are not looking just to teach educated people. We want everyone to know it is important to have our language. And to help them discover that sense of identity, that being a Yakama is important. We want to get everyone interested in it.

Rose and Roger now work within the public school system on the reservation, teaching language to elementary, middle, and high school students. In this way, they are actively seeking to address the soul wounds that have stripped our people of our language use, knowledge, and traditions. They extend the benefits of the Yakama-NILI partnership to a broader group of tribal peoples by implementing what they have learned at NILI into classrooms on the reservation. This is an applied example of decolonization that actively subverts a settler-colonial education agenda that, historically, has forbidden the teaching of indigenous languages and traditions within the schools. Rose and Roger are leaders in this effort, humbly following in the footsteps of elders such as Virginia and Patsy, who tirelessly work to ensure the language and cultural teachings continue to be shared across the generations.

Unanimously, the people I interviewed stated that their work with the language was important because of the intergenerational responsibility that is inherent within our culture. In short, they were actively working to revitalize the language because of instructions that elders had provided. And, they felt a responsibility to learn and teach all they could so that the future generations would have a greater connection and sense of empowerment with their language.

For example, I asked Virginia how she got started doing her work with the language. She shared:

> Well, I got started when my stepfather asked me to continue his work. He was involved in developing, well, I guess his thought was to develop a dictionary of some sort, you know, so he started out by training five women, five Indian women. And he was still on the Tribal Council, matter of fact, he was the Chairman. He used to take time in the evening to teach five women how to read and write the language after he got together with Dr. Rigsby [a linguist], and he learned how to read and write the alphabet. So that is what he was teaching the women. But I wasn't involved at all. I had my own occupation. I was a medical record librarian and I worked in the hospital. I worked in Sunnyside and that's where I lived. I'd come home now and then and visit and you know, and he got sick. He had a heart problem. And he got worse and worse and finally he told me, "I would like you to take up my work. Go back to school and get a degree in anthropology and continue my work." Evidently, he was told that the only background you could have for that would be anthropology and I didn't care for anthropology at all because of the stigma, you know, at that time, where people were digging Indian graves and the Indian people were very unhappy about it, and so was I. And, I kind of struggled with it. I didn't want to. But he kept it up and finally he got really sick. And he gave me a very serious talk about how people are only talking English now and later on there won't be anybody talking Indian anymore. I got to thinking about it because we all spoke Indian at home, everybody. And well, I finally did go back to school in Ellensburg at Central Washington University and I struggled with it. I mean my attitude about anthropology didn't help. But then I began to get acquainted with people who helped me.

In Virginia's narrative, she acknowledges the difficulties involved with seeking out training to become skilled in documenting, preserving, and revitalizing one's indigenous language. Although she was a fluent Ichish-kíin speaker, she still struggled with seeking out a formal university education, but persisted because it was part of the instructions her stepfather provided to her. Virginia did not have the typical "traditional" college-age student profile. She was a military veteran, was already in the full-time workforce, and was the first generation to attend college in her family. She remembers the difficulties involved in going to college and doing a course of study she did not completely understand. Yet she persisted because of her stepfather's serious talk about the ways our language was threatened. Virginia's narrative has an urgent message about survivance—"people are only talking English now and later on there won't be anybody talking Indian anymore"—and she realized it would take a tremendous effort to disrupt the pattern of language loss and assimilation among our people. Virginia trusted in the words of her beloved elder and, perhaps ironically, started taking university classes in anthropology, a discipline fraught with assimilationist and settler-colonial projects. Although she struggled to accept this challenge, Virginia persisted on the difficult journey and eventually found people who understood her educational mission and supported her work with encouraging words and helpful networking connections. Ultimately, Virginia refined her skills in formal linguistics, and she completed her stepfather's work on writing a practical dictionary of the Yakama language (Beavert and Rigsby 1975). This lengthy document served as the basis for emerging language classes in and around the reservation. Countless photocopies circulate among tribal peoples and scholars interested in our language. In discussing this landmark document, Virginia is always quick to credit the vision and work of her stepfather, who foresaw the difficulties of our people to keep our language.

At the heart of each language revitalization activist's narrative is an unwavering dedication to the practical, to the applied. Virginia shared with me that she learned her practical approach to language revitalization work from another elder. Early in Virginia's involvement as a leader in these efforts, she was at an indigenous language conference. She spoke freely to the group about the challenges of doing this work, the lack of resources, the numerous barriers, and so on. Then, one elder jumped up, pointed at her, and let her know how much potential she had, how important her work was, and gave her a simple message that Virginia has forever carried with her. That message was "Just do it!" When Virginia tells this story, she giggles with delight, remembering that elder jumping and pointing at her.

She said it startled her, but she knew he was right. Doing the work was what mattered. This message represents the spirit of her work. She told me, "Ever since then, I've been trying to do it every way I can." Virginia was one of the few interviewees who was not averse to the term "activist" in describing her work with language and culture. When I asked her why she considered herself a language revitalization activist, she simply responded, "I don't want our language to die!"

Virginia's approach to language revitalization is rooted in her strong belief that tribal peoples themselves must take responsibility for upholding our traditions. She believes we cannot rely on government entities, including tribal governments, to solve our problems for us. Virginia's leadership in the language revitalization movement is rooted in what Begay, Cornell, Jorgensen, and Pryor have identified as the most valuable contribution of Native leaders: imagining a new situation to believe things can be different, and then working to make things different (Begay et al. 2007).

Virginia served as an elected official to the Yakama Nation General Council for many years, but now in her "retirement years," she prefers to work at the grassroots level: teaching classes, mentoring younger people who wish to learn the language (adapting master-apprentice methodologies), writing (lesson plans, stories, legends, and new entries for the next version of the Ichishkíin dictionary), and being willing to meet and share materials with anyone who has a genuine interest in learning the language. The grassroots approach that Virginia embraces is particularly important because of a general lack of formal institutional support for language work. Indigenous language revitalization efforts are usually poorly resourced, with activists scrambling to seek support from their tribes, educational institutions, government agencies, and nonprofit organizations. Oftentimes, these agencies and institutions have little or no formal support to offer. Virginia talked about these challenges, noting that she had to seek support outside of her tribal government structure. This decision was difficult, as Virginia was raised in the traditional way, and some tribal elders believed the language should not be spoken, taught, or shared with outsiders. Virginia shared how her work with non-tribal peoples caused some conflict within her family:

> My mother didn't really approve of that [working with non-tribal peoples], until she went to the university in Canada with me. She went along to buy herself a Canadian blanket. And so she said let's take my motor home and go up there, because Sharon [linguistics professor at the University of Washington] and I were scheduled to

do a demonstration. Well, she listened, and half of the audience was Indian and the other half was linguists. Canadian Indians came in and talked about the problems they were having, losing their language and their culture, and they needed help and things. Then the linguists were discussing, you know, how to strategize academia on trying to help the tribes at that time.

And my mother was sitting in her wheelchair and she had her head hanging *way* down like she was asleep. And then Sharon and I did our part of the demonstration about what we're doing to try to help you know, things to get going.

And we did my part and she did her part and we kind of put it together and how we're trying to do this. I talked about how the language was, the alphabet was developed and the man that helped us moved to Australia. And then my stepfather died and that kind of left the work undone. And how he made me go back to school and try to pick it up again and how Sharon had trained me to use the computer and the font, and everything in the computer. [I shared how] I was trying to do it and I discussed that with them, and told them this is how they could do it—to demonstrate how *they* could do it. And then Sharon did her share on how she was trying to help me. And how the university was getting involved and helping, you know, not helping, but giving her support to do it. And so we were putting all this together and then how it could work. The other linguists started talking about how it could work with the Canadians, you know.

After the presentation we had lunch and I took [my mother] back to where I got her an apartment on the campus. Then she said, "Well, I never realized how important this work was that you're doing." She said, "From now on I'm going to support you and help you out, you know, when you need help."

Virginia's mother was initially unsupportive of Virginia's work with non-Indian linguists. However, after attending a conference in which she began to understand the critical nature of Virginia's work, she changed her view and offered support and approval. This story is deeply meaningful to Virginia, as she had, before that conference, struggled with the conflicting messages she received about the important language work that she was doing. On the one hand, her stepfather had "made her" go back to school to be formally trained in linguistics, so that she could partner with linguists in order to save the language. Yet on the other hand, her mother disapproved and refused to help answer questions that Virginia had when she was doing her work with the language. After the conference, Virginia's mother's heart softened. Being in that auditorium, seeing how special and useful Virginia's work was, not only to her own people, but to the First Nations people who looked to her for guidance, Virginia's mother realized that her daughter's work indeed merited as much support as possible. Her humble message to Virginia was, "I'm going to support you and help you out."

This gesture of support was important emotionally, but also practically, as Virginia's mother knew things that could help Virginia's work by laying out some of the background to specific terms within the language. Virginia shared the meaning of this:

> Because before that [time when Virginia's mother was supportive] I would ask her questions and she would say, "Well, you're the expert!" You know, "you should know."
>
> Then after that [conference in Canada] she would elaborate on some things that, well, you know, I'm just like the rest of the young people. I know some things, but I don't know the background to how this came about! You know, the *old* background. Well she helped explain some of these things to me, the way she was told.
>
> And so that's why I always say I don't know everything. And you know, and it just gives me incentive to go out and activate as much interest as possible.

As the leader of the Ichishkíin language revitalization movement, Virginia serves her people with a strong sense of humility. She is always quick to remind people that she does not "know everything" but she only knows "what her elders taught her." In this way, she claims her rightful leadership role, but she also refuses to be "the" authority, leaving space for other elders and adults who wish to also serve as leaders. This tradition, of claiming one's knowledge, rooted in the teachings of one's elders, is a proud and strong indigenous epistemological tradition, yet it resists the Western tendency to equate leadership and knowledge with a totalizing knowledge discourse (Jacob 2012). Virginia's leadership provides an example of what indigenous legal scholar Rebecca Tsosie (2007) has termed an "intercultural framework" that honors group-oriented and collective ownership, as Virginia insists that she is not all-knowing, nor does the knowledge originate with her, but rather she is simply the holder of knowledge that her elders shared with her. Virginia's humble attitude reminds us that indigenous knowledge systems are rooted in the group's collective past. As such,

Virginia refuses to claim that she speaks for all people, or that she knows everything about Ichishkíin. She is, however, quick to share stories and teachings with students and people who are eager and sincere about wanting to learn. At her core, she is a loving teacher who has a very practical approach to doing her work.

Building a Moral Community

Within the narratives about the Yakama-NILI partnership is a rich understanding about the stakes of building a moral community that is centered on meeting tribal peoples' needs. For example, Greg shared the importance of NILI in sparking his imagination about collaborative work that could make an impact in Ichishkíin language preservation and revitalization. Speaking about the first time he attended the NILI summer institute, he shared:

> That's where I met Janne Underriner, Scott Delancy, all the people down there, and I really, that's what really got me interested in University of Oregon down there because they were doing a lot of stuff. I met a lot of people besides myself and Virginia that were really interested in revitalizing, preserving the language. And a lot of people who were interested in helping us, so we had people who taught us how to do teaching methods so that, when we teach in the community, we could do a better job. We had people showing us how, teaching us linguistics, and for some people this is like elders and stuff, coming with the language, or coming to NILI, and you know, they are starting to learn about linguistics. They are completely fluent in their language, but they didn't know how to describe some of the rules, or you know, "Why is this showing up now, but it's not showing up there?" "Why does this sound change when it used to be this sound?" And those are stuff that you don't know. It's internal, internalized, and you can't really explain it unless you're a linguist and you know these linguistic rules. So they helped the elders with that. And you know we also learned about databases and storing our recordings and for ways to do that type of stuff and how do you utilize technology and so that whole experience, I did that [attended NILI] two years.

Greg's comments clarify the importance of having a critical mass of people who are dedicated to language revitalization. Within the summer institute, Greg saw that the focus was on developing and providing tools that tribal community members needed to do the language work themselves. Thus, at the heart of the partnership effort is the goal of tribal self-determination. This model of education inspired Greg to follow the lead of his elder, Virginia. Greg is now also enrolled in the doctoral program in linguistics at the University of Oregon. Like Virginia, Greg is focusing his dissertation on Ichishkíin. Their scholarship will add to our assets in the movement to revitalize our indigenous language.

The Yakama-NILI partnership was initially built around the NILI Summer Institute, a two-week intensive course hosted on the University of Oregon campus. In my interview with Dr. Janne Underriner, the director of NILI, I asked her how the Summer Institute got started. Her comments make clear that tribal people's vision of community empowerment is what guides all of the work. Janne shared that the formal beginning of NILI could be traced back to a meeting between tribal community members and University of Oregon linguistics graduate students and professors. She shared that at the meeting, tribal peoples expressed their needs:

> They wanted within their communities more language classes, community language classes, language taught in schools or Head Start programs or developing more community schools. So we met with them and then we started NILI that summer.

I asked Janne about the actual process of starting NILI. She insisted it was an uncomplicated process, relying only on sincere outreach among existing networks of tribal peoples, careful listening to tribal community needs, and dedication to actively addressing those needs. I asked her to share more details. She responded:

> Well, really we sat for one day, we convened, I don't remember the date but it was in May and we *really* listened. And I was the note keeper and I was nervous because I knew I had to just get it right, about what people's needs were. I mean it was really, it was actually that simple . . . at this kind of symposium or gathering. All these folks came together . . . Warm Springs and Umatilla . . . And Wendell and Thomas said, "Let's do it" and "Let's get it going." And so we did. I mean we listened to them. We made it happen.

The first NILI Summer Institute took place in 1996. The foundational meeting that Janne describes above took place in May, and the Summer

Institute took place that same summer, less than two months later. After listening to tribal people's needs, Janne took the lead to organize support for the Summer Institute on campus, getting support from summer housing programs, instructors from the linguistics department, and support from diversity and equity offices. Working with a shoestring budget, Janne found a way to host the institute and charge modest tuition and room and board charges, which attendees paid for out of pocket or with support from their tribes. I asked Janne how she was able to pull together a Summer Institute in just a few weeks.

MJ: So you organized that quickly?

JANNE: We did. Because those of us that, that really had an applied specialty had taught language and had taught second language acquisition which is what we thought folks needed, and taught teaching methods. And some of us had taught linguistics so it's not like we didn't have that expertise that we were really able to do that. And the first year, well, for the first many years, we went three weeks . . . I won't say it was unorganized because it was actually very organized but we were so inexperienced.

MJ: It sounds very grassroots, right? Not bogged down with university bureaucracy.

JANNE: It had *nothing* to do with university bureaucracy. The *tribes* wanted it. We said we're going to do it . . . That was what, fourteen years ago now . . . There were thirteen of us [that first year], more than I thought would come. And it was fabulous . . . mostly folks in their forties, fifties, and sixties that wanted to learn more about how the language worked and how they could teach. All of them had been teaching at some point. So you know, that is exactly what we did. We had dinners at my house. We had meetings at my house. We learned how to make fry bread [laughter].

MJ: There was no NILI office then or anything?

JANNE: No.

After the initial start of the Summer Institute, Janne began assessing ways it could be improved, to better serve tribal peoples' needs:

So I went out and met more with the tribes. I mean something worked and we were together and it was actually really a wonderful experience and it was heartfelt if it was anything. I mean, it took two years to learn that folks don't really need a theoretical class in second language acquisition. It's not what folks that want to be language teachers really need to get themselves going. They really need to know how to develop materials and what teaching techniques work in different situations. They just really need this nice package, or these tools, or whatever that they keep in their pockets that they can pull out and go, "This is what I need now." And it's really what NILI needs to be about and what it's morphed into. So the following year, almost everybody who came the first year came the second year with an addition of a few other people.

Janne took on the main responsibility of planning and coordinating the Summer Institute. She was supported by a part-time graduate teaching fellowship position, which she was grateful to have, but many people realized that in order to sustain and grow NILI, a greater level of support was needed. Janne shared some of the complications of running the institute without strong structural support:

So that was clearly the motivating factor in us really working to look for funding and write grants and, because, once I graduated I was basically the joke at the university, with even the president was, I mean NILI was basically the back seat of my car. I mean, it was my car or it was my dining room. Those of us at NILI would affectionately call it 113-B or something in the EMU [student union building], which was the center building. We would always sit at this one table on the south side in the EMU, because it has this beautiful window that looks out onto the trees in this little park area there, it's just pretty every season. And then there's this little closet that's there, it's marked 113-A or whatever it is. That was the joke, the NILI office was in the EMU [in the common area] right across from [the utility closet] 113.

Janne shared that NILI, in her opinion, was "started by the tribes." She insisted, "We didn't start NILI. We were here at the university . . . we listened . . . and some of us just really didn't walk away from it." NILI eventually was able to move out of the "imaginary office" at the student union building. In the 2006–2007 school year, NILI was provided office space in a university-owned house adjacent to the campus. Clearly, a long-term commitment to developing and sustaining tribal partnerships is an important part of NILI's model. This community-based vision guided the work of NILI regardless of the amount of resources the university provided.

Another major aspect of the NILI model is the recognition that supporting tribal self-determination means having tribal peoples present within the partnership. Evidence of a successful partnership means Native peoples will be on campus, accessing the resources of the university for their own growth and development, with the goal of benefiting their home tribal communities. Janne reflected on this, sharing the two most important developments on campus: 1) the structural support of developing a director's position, to ensure the long-term viability of NILI, and 2) supporting Native graduate students. Janne views the presence of Native graduate students as key to the success of their partnerships. One of the most significant accomplishments is the fact that NILI helped to recruit and retain Virginia Beavert to reenter school at the University of Oregon, to earn a PhD in linguistics. Janne shared her view of the significance of having a revered elder as a valued partner, graduate student, and mentor:

> I feel like in her being here she has the ability to help us mold, help us explore, help us figure out better ways to work with the tribes and be better nurturers and providers and professors and teachers and instructors and all of that for Native students. And I think the larger picture is for all students. Because she's very much that way. She's very inclusive.

Janne's quote reflects the humility that is woven throughout all of her work at NILI. Janne holds a PhD in linguistics, is the co-founder of NILI, and serves as the director of NILI at the University of Oregon. Rather than viewing tribal peoples as "lucky" to be able to access the resources at the university, she sees herself as fortunate to work with and learn from them. Within her quote, there is a deep sense of responsibility toward the tribal peoples who choose to work with NILI.

Roger reflected on the significance of a university reaching out and truly valuing the presence of a tribal elder:

> I mean if the University of Oregon can make Tuxámshish feel comfortable and get her to go there, I mean it was easy for me . . . I mean, those people at Oregon, whatever they're doing, I haven't put a whole lot of thought into it, but if other universities are serious

about it, well there's a model. And it's not just you know the institution it's the people and you've got to know how to act. That NILI, it's not just there in Oregon where we go to them. They come here. I would say . . . probably about monthly . . . they come here and they train our people, how to be teachers and hopefully how to record. They write the grants and I help write the grants now, because they trained me . . . Hopefully if we have people that have a solid understanding of the linguistics and know what some other model programs are doing out there we can get things turned around.

Roger's narrative helps us understand the importance of a university doing community-based outreach and partnership-building. Central to the success of the Yakama-NILI partnership is the fact that university personnel visit and host tribal peoples. NILI personnel are willing to meet community members' needs and allow tribal needs to shape the partnership agenda. Empowering tribal peoples to do language revitalization work is a major emphasis of the partnership. This focus on community empowerment is important within an activist scholarship agenda, a point that I discuss in more detail in chapter 5, when I outline recommendations for university personnel and tribal community members wishing to collaborate on activist scholarship projects.

The Yakama-NILI partnership promotes a vibrant form of community-empowered language revitalization. As such, it is supporting a grassroots effort to revive Yakama cultural traditions. Yet, most interviewees were hesitant to define themselves as "activists," as they were worried that the term would have undesirable political connotations. I asked Joana Jansen, a project coordinator for NILI, if she considered herself a language revitalization activist. At first, she mentioned that the term might be loaded in some contexts, but then she concluded with her own definition of what a language revitalization activist is, which she embraced. She later expanded on her comments to reinforce her point that language revitalization work must be done with love. In fact, Joana views her work as a blessing in her life:

> In terms of that word [activist] being used as someone who cares about a language, who cares about the future of the language and who is devoting time and work and energy and love to that language, yes, I'm a language activist . . . And I care about the people. I think when I started I didn't know how much it was about people. I mean,

I look at language and this book is full of language and sentences and oh they're cool and I love them, I can read them and break them down into little pieces. But it's about the relationships and when I started working with NILI, I didn't know that. I didn't know that I was going to meet people that were going to change my life, for the rest of my life . . . and that's another blessing of this work . . . to reiterate the privilege and the honor that I have, in being able to do what I'm doing. I feel very lucky and very blessed in this . . . I just feel lucky. It's not something I was looking for, or you know, it's not something I was seeking after or thought would happen but it's just been, it's just added so much richness, to do this work.

One of the lessons of the NILI model is that an indigenous-centered education has benefits beyond indigenous communities. That is, the intellectual project of participating in Ichishkíin language documentation and revitalization serves as a scholarly contribution as well as social justice praxis toward building a "moral community" that recognizes the inherent worth of indigenous languages as invaluable contributions to a society that values diverse worldviews (McCarty 2011, 16; Meek 2009, 166–167). Non-Indians who are a part of the Yakama-NILI partnership noted how their lives were changed by working with the language, Virginia, and NILI. The relationships they built with Yakama peoples were some of the most meaningful in their lives. Above I noted that Joana counts her work with Yakama peoples and Ichishkíin as a blessing. Similarly, Regan Anderson, an undergraduate linguistics student at the University of Oregon, counts her work with NILI and Virginia as the most significant part of her educational career. She is planning to continue on to graduate school in linguistics, hoping to dedicate her life to Ichishkíin revitalization. I asked her how she got involved in this work. She explained that she was feeling lost in her educational pathway, so she decided to take a quarter off to carefully think through her educational options and what she wanted to do with her life. Once she stepped foot into Virginia's Sahaptin classroom upon returning, she knew she was in the right place. Regan shared:

> I was trying to decide [what to major in]. I took a cultural anthropology class and it kind of opened my eyes to endangered languages, just talking about linguistic anthropology. So I started kind of looking into endangered languages and saw the National Geographic map of the places in the world that there is most need of research, and Washington and Oregon happened to be one of those places. So

I stated emailing linguistics people here. And eventually I got Janne's name and heard that Virginia would be teaching Sahaptin and I was trying to decide if I should change my major or not from architecture to linguistics. And I actually took a term off, the fall term, to just think about it. And then, I ended up getting Joana's name and emailed her about adding the class [Sahaptin 102] late after missing a term [Sahaptin 101]. And they let me in and said, "If you can catch up you can stay." . . . I made so many little flash cards and I labeled [with Sahaptin words and phrases] my entire house and my room. Yeah, just walking in and seeing Virginia and Roger and Joana, it just kind of felt like the right place to be, so I worked really hard . . . So that's how it came about . . . I really found my heart here at NILI. And, everybody here is just so kind and the language itself, there's so much kindness in the language that it gets lost in English. And the perspective of it has really touched my heart in a way that I didn't know there was that depth until I started learning this language. And everybody that I've met that's been associated with it has had that kindness, too . . . And so, yeah, it just feels like such important work and that kind of adds to the enthusiasm, motivation, and it just has brought my life so much depth to be part of this. I feel really blessed.

Regan views her work with Ichishkíin as a blessing. She shared that learning Ichishkíin helped her see the importance of the worldview and the culture that is embedded within the language. Regan looked to a National Geographic map to better understand the crisis of global indigenous language loss. Much to her surprise, she was attending college in one of the regions needing research to help ensure indigenous cultural survival. She felt drawn to learn from Virginia and other students and teachers who were already engaged in building a movement around teaching and learning Ichishkíin. In so doing, she learned a new worldview that changed her life. Regan's narrative helps demonstrate the importance of indigenous-centered education and the possibilities for building a moral community. Not only is Regan learning valuable academic skills and a subject matter that empowers her, but she is also learning how to apply these skills in a way that empowers indigenous peoples. In her words, her role in the Yakama-NILI partnership has brought "so much depth" to her life. I asked her to explain this, and she responded:

What gave me the ability to kind of see it was actually just the other day in a Summer Institute language class. Arlita [an elder language teacher attending the Summer Institute] was talking, and she was talking about redirecting children. And, I think it started because somebody said, "How do you say this English sentence in Ichish-kíin?" [to reprimand a child]. And Arlita and Virginia both were saying, "You know, we can *translate* your English sentence into Ich-ishkíin, but it won't be true Ichishkíin because we wouldn't say that normally. We wouldn't even put that sentence together, really." And it led into an example of when you redirect children, you frame it in a way, you don't say, ["don't do this"]. You say [in a kind voice], "Rather, do it like this" [Arlita demonstrated this with one of the student's children, lovingly stroking the child's hair.] And you are very loving with them.

One of my favorite things about languages is the perspectives that you get, and the world view that you get, and how a culture and people embrace life itself. I just found in this language [Ichishkíin], things are framed with such kindness, and you can feel it when you're talking to these people. And Virginia, you know, my first thought was it's just Virginia [who is kind]. And then I meet some-body else and, oh, my goodness, you are the most kind person, too. The deeper I get into learning Ichishkíin, and the way that it is struc-tured, it's just softer and more peaceful, and you can't even convey anger in the same way that you can in English. You know, you can definitely get your point across, and there are ways for things, but they're not the English way. And just, see, there's just more, I don't know, a softer embrace of individual people and hearts. And there's just this element of almost collaboration. Yeah, I don't know how to explain it.

Regan's description of what it means to learn Ichishkíin is a narrative that is full of gratitude. She struggled to find the exact English words that would convey her sense of respect for her teachers and fellow students. She understands that cultural teachings are embedded within the lan-guage. Everyday phrases and instructions are delivered and structured in a manner absolutely distinct from "the English way," as Regan states. Be-cause of the richness of the teachings and the importance of revitalizing this precious language, Regan feels drawn to work with Ichishkíin for the rest of her life. This is a bold decision being made by a non-Indian under-graduate student. Initially, Regan's family did not understand her interest in Ichishkíin. She shared:

At first they [family members] made fun of me, asking "What are you going to do with an endangered language? What's the point? You can't speak to anyone!" And now they understand and they're all really interested. I think it's opened their eyes, too, to the importance of it. Yeah, so they've come to be really supportive of it.

Regan recalls the confusion her family members felt about her studying an endangered language, wondering what she would do with such an education. "What's the point? You can't speak to anyone" follows the logic that unfortunately proves true often enough, that endangered languages will die through a process of cultural and physical genocide of indigenous peoples. Yet, through her involvement with a community-based language revitalization project, Regan has learned that cultural survival is possible. This process has helped her transform her educational and vocational pathway, and she is a crucial part of building a moral community within the Yakama-NILI partnership. Along this journey, she has also helped to teach her own family about the importance of indigenous language revitalization, and thus brought them into the fold of the larger project that builds a moral community concerned with Yakama language revitalization. In the process, Regan has confronted questions about what the role of non-Indians might be for addressing problems rooted in a colonial past. Regan's response has been to support elders and community members, as they define the best approaches for engaging in language revitalization work. Through her involvement, Regan has received a "new perspective," and she feels "blessed" to have learned about the inherent value of Ichishkíin as a worldview. The benefits of Regan's indigenous language education helps to demonstrate the importance of an indigenous-centered education for non-Native peoples, and Regan has effectively taught her family members that losing an indigenous language will be a loss to everyone; in Regan's words, her family now understands the "importance of it." The moral community that the Yakama-NILI partnership provides is one in which all peoples who are concerned about language revitalization can find a place to participate, grow, and learn as a person. As such, the partnership represents a commitment to healing. The language knowledge gaps within the Yakama community are evidence of the soul wound of colonialism, and the strong, empowering efforts of language revitalization taking place are evidence of healing for our peoples. Regan's narrative represents how non-Native students benefit from an indigenous-centered education that is only possible because of the strong partnership between tribal peoples and universities. This is a point I discuss further in chapter 5, where I propose recommendations for successful partnership-building.

Developing a Culturally Relevant Representation of the Yakama-NILI Partnership Model

This chapter has examined the ways in which activists engage in language revitalization within the Yakama-NILI partnership. I have developed a list of ten principles that define the essence of the activists' work. Below I provide the list of principles, as well as, in figure 3, a culturally relevant figure that represents the principles as a cohesive whole.

Principles of the Yakama-NILI model:

1. Support intergenerational teaching and learning
2. Collaborate to create critical mass
3. Develop practical, applied focus
4. View work in spiritual terms
5. Listen
6. Practice sincere outreach
7. Encourage long-term commitment
8. Support solution oriented Do-ing
9. Support grassroots efforts
10. Aim all efforts at supporting tribal peoples' self-determination

Cultural Relevance of Figure 3

I choose to represent the visual model as a culturally relevant image. K'úsi (horse) has great meaning to Yakama peoples. Yakama elders often share stories of the importance of horses to our people's survival. In this book's introduction, I shared tribal histories that explain horses are a gift from the Creator. Today, large herds of wild horses still remain on the reservation foothills, and careful management of them as a precious resource is one of the most important issues facing our natural resources personnel (Yakama Nation 2012). Most of all, however, Virginia Beavert inspired the use of the horse as the basis of the model because of her extensive knowledge of horses and the many stories she tells about this beloved animal.

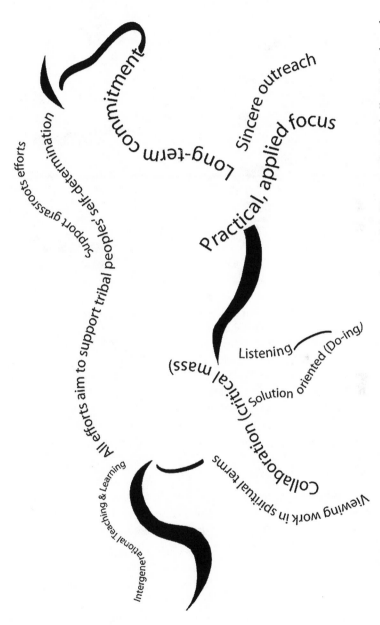

Sincere outreach

Long-term commitment

Practical, applied focus

Support grassroots efforts

Support tribal peoples' self-determination

All efforts aim to support tribal peoples' self-determination

Listening

Solution oriented (Do-ing)

Collaboration (critical mass)

Viewing work in spiritual terms

Intergenerational Teaching & Learning

Figure 3. Yakama-Northwest Indian Language Institute partnership model. (Drawing by Michelle M. Jacob and Christopher J. Andersen)

Figure 4. NILI attendees and Farewell dancers (described in the opening of chapter 2) at the longhouse on the University of Oregon campus during the 2011 NILI Summer Institute. Three interviewees are pictured, including Joana (third from left), Virginia (fourth from left), and Regan (fifth from left). The author is second from left. (Photo by Christopher J. Andersen)

As the image shows, movement is important in this model. Language revitalization work, like k'úsi, adapts and moves through the environment. The essence of this model is rooted in the knowledge gained through the NILI-Yakama case study, as well as the rich body of literature that has developed around Indian education scholarship over the past forty years, which demands that educational systems recognize the inherent cultural and political rights that indigenous peoples hold. Education systems must value and support tribal peoples' vision of self-determination. The ten principles represented in the model provide insight into how this process can work in a partnership between educational institutions and tribal partners. Yet, not all of the examples of indigenous education activism take place in partnerships with formal education systems. In the next chapter, we will examine a case study of grassroots activism that articulates a model of cultural revitalization outside of the formal schooling system.

CHAPTER THREE

Think of the Seven Generations

Xwayamamí Ishích

Old Ways of Preserving Fish: An Ethnographic Note about Lessons from the Ancestors

*　　*　　*

It is a beautiful late-summer day with clear blue skies and warm, bright sunshine. The sun's rays are so warm and comfortable, it seems almost as if the sun is smiling down upon us. Today we will learn how to care for food as a gift from the Creator, and in doing so, we will understand how much we depend on the sun (*áan*) and the wind (*hulí*). These are the lessons of our ancestors. We are fortunate that elders have carried these lessons and are ready to share them with us. The younger generations are ready to learn and will in turn become the next teachers for the future generations.

We drive up the long, bumpy dirt driveway, careful to avoid the adjacent irrigation ditch that waters nearby pastures. As I look upon the abundant plant life on the shoulders of the deep ditch, my mind drifts; I think back to the countless hours I have spent in the library, examining the archives of local newspapers from over 100 years ago. I recall the dramatic nineteenth century headlines of the white-owned media, which tittered with delight about the riches that could be made if further settlement were allowed onto the reservation. The headlines called for opening the Yakama Reservation, the rich land being "wasted" by "lazy" and "ignorant"

Indians, who resisted the commands of the settlers, missionaries, and War Department officials, all of whom insisted that Yakamas give up their "blanket lives" for a more civilized ranching and farming existence.

Back in the twenty-first century, bumping along on the remote dirt road on the reservation, I think of how the irrigation ditch beside me is a link to that past, how the man-made veins of water have brought new patterns of life to the reservation. I think about how our people have adapted and changed over the past hundred years.

As we continue up the road, swerving to miss the largest holes, I also think about the Indian family who is hosting us today. They use their plot of land on the Yakama Reservation to engage in an act of resistance. They see their land as a base for activities that encourage and inspire cultural revitalization. They use Facebook and word-of-mouth advertising to invite strangers and friends into their home to build a collective of intergenerational teachers and learners—to ensure the old ways, the traditional teachings, will not be lost.

Out in the dirt area beside the overgrown field, the air is calm and quiet. A dozen adults gather around the wooden table, quietly greeting each other and softly shaking hands. Ten or so children play in the nearby garden and on the swing set adjacent to the house. Soon the elder emerges from the house, coffee cup in hand, and greets the newcomers. She moves a lawn chair into the shade and begins chatting with those who gather around her. She gives the update of how the fish are doing. She is pleased with the work that the group did yesterday, carefully learning the little-known fillet technique required for wind-drying fish. Several young women laugh quietly, recounting how difficult this fillet technique was, and they make fun of their misshapen fillets, which are now hanging (somewhat lopsidedly) in the wind-drying shed. The elder smiles, laughs politely, and reassures the women they are doing well. As beginners, they cannot expect to have perfect, symmetrical fillets. Such fine work takes years of practice. Some of the children and adults want to visit the fish. We go inside the wind-drying shed. The fresh smell of fish is strong and delicious. "Stand back a little bit!" we instruct one eager young girl. We tell her if she stands too close, the fat from the rich fish will drip on her head. We point to the ground, showing her all the droplets of rich salmon and steelhead oil already rendered from the fillets. The elder watches us, giggling at the young girl, perhaps recalling a time, over fifty years ago, when she was in the young's girl's place, eager and curious, dodging rendering fat in the drying shed, and listening to the gentle scolding of adults watching over her.

The elder joins us in the shed, examining the fillets. "Yes, this is good," she tells us. "The fat needs to drip out so the fish can dry and not spoil," she explains. We nod our heads in understanding. "You can taste a little bit if you like," she tells us. She breaks off a tiny piece and eats it, showing us the appropriate size to taste. The young girls in the shed are excited to taste the fish, telling us, "I want to taste it!" We help them get small pieces, and then help ourselves to a tiny bite-sized piece. The fish is rich, oily, and fresh. Its strong flavor is delicious. "Mmmm!" I say. "It is rich!" The young girls echo my compliments, and their eager little voices ask for more fish.

The elder smiles at the fresh taste of the fish, and she nods in agreement. "Don't eat too much," she warns. "It will go right through you. That is why we need to let the fat drip."

We nod quietly, showing we are listening. The elder wants to make sure we understand, so she adds, "If you eat too much now, you will be on the toilet all day!" Then she giggles softly.

We giggle with the elder. I am touched by the way the elder's eyes light up with life when she tells stories and speaks from the heart. She is so giving and kind; all of the people, gathered in the dirt area that day, next to the overgrown field, are eager to learn from this generous elder. The warm sunshine continues to smile down upon us, providing a good day to dry fish. In the afternoon, the wind will come, and together the wind and sun will help us dry all these fillets, which will be stored away until it is time for the elders' winter giveaway. We stand quietly for a moment in the shed, admiring the Creator's gift of bountiful fish. A meadowlark sings in the distance. It is a happy, spiritual moment in the drying shed, with the fish oil dripping down beside us.

✻   ✻   ✻

Background and Purpose of X̱wayamamí Ishích

X̱wayamamí Ishích is a nonprofit organization based on the Yakama Reservation and co-founded by a husband and wife team, Greg (whom readers met in chapter 2) and Jessica Sutterlict. Compared to the other case studies in this book, X̱wayamamí Ishích has a much younger history, receiving official 501(c)3 status in Washington State in 2007. The organization has peaks of activity during Yakama traditional foods harvesting seasons, such as during the spring and fall salmon runs on the Columbia River. X̱wayamamí Ishích is an example of a grassroots organization developing partnerships and methodologies to create an indigenous-centered educational model that revitalizes cultural practices without the benefit of an educational institutional home. As such, the nonprofit is largely operated out of Greg and Jessica's home on the reservation. Their kitchen table serves as the main headquarters and offers a meeting area and workspace. Stretching their limited resources, activists involved with X̲wayamamí Ishích have creatively worked with other organizations on the reservation. For example, X̲wayamamí Ishích has collaborated with the Yakama Nation Tribal School to bring a busload of children to one of their salmon smoking workshops. Additionally, the Yakama Nation Fisheries and Yakama Nation Forest Products offices have given in-kind donations to support X̲wayamamí Ishích workshops. Finally, the organization is beginning to seek small grants, and their traditional foods workshops are supported by an award from Winona LaDuke's organization, Honor the Earth.

Similar to participants in previous case studies covered in earlier chapters, activists involved in X̲wayamamí Ishích viewed their work as fulfilling a responsibility to promote intergenerational teaching and learning. Activists viewed elders and youth as particularly important in this process, due to the elders holding traditional knowledge and the youth serving as the future teachers of this knowledge. In this chapter, I draw from interviews I conducted with the X̲wayamamí Ishích president (Jessica) and vice president (Greg) along with a tribal elder (Ramona) who collaborates with X̲wayamamí Ishích to offer traditional foods workshops on the reservation. Their narratives emphasize two important themes: 1) The Seven Generations philosophy guides their activist work. 2) Women are important culture bearers in grassroots cultural revitalization efforts. I analyze these themes to articulate the ways that indigenous grassroots activism can help us work toward dismantling colonial logics and conclude by sharing my illustration, in figure 6, of the theoretical model that underlies the activist work of X̲wayamamí Ishích. In so doing, my analysis contributes to our understanding of indigenous social change and advances the scholarship on decolonization through articulating a theory of Yakama cultural revitalization.

Prophecy of the Seven Generations

In our every deliberation, we must consider the impact of our decisions on the next seven generations.
FROM THE GREAT LAW OF THE IROQUOIS CONFEDERACY

The Seven Generations prophecy is important in many indigenous communities. Intergenerational teaching is important for encouraging current generations to think about their actions with a long-term and communally based vision. Such a vision has inspired countless indigenous and non-indigenous peoples. The founders of the nonprofit organization X̱wayamamí Ishích discussed the Seven Generations philosophy as an important motivation for their activist work. They viewed the Seven Generations philosophy as a directive to build upon the past wisdom and teachings of the previous generations, as well as to dedicate their efforts to supporting the future generations. Since 2010, a major way that X̱wayamamí Ishích accomplishes this is by offering seasonal workshops that bring elders and youth together to teach community members about traditional food gathering and preservation.

Indigenous cultural revitalization efforts depend on intergenerational teaching and learning; it is a form of education that is rarely featured in Western educational systems. Tribal elders privilege oral histories, as opposed to textbooks, as part of the teachings they learned from a previous generation of elders. In this educational process, children and young adults must have blocks of time to spend with elders, as teachings take place through storytelling, teaching by example, and learning through repetition. If this indigenous cultural educational transmission is broken, then gaps will emerge, with the potential for cultural knowledge to be completely disrupted. Once knowledge gaps set in, even for just one generation, the cultural teachings are difficult to revive. One of the X̱wayamamí Ishích founders, Greg Sutterlict, discusses this point in his interview, in terms of his motivation to do cultural revitalization work. He connects his work with X̱wayamamí Ishích to the language revitalization work he does with the Northwest Indian Language Institute (see chapter 2). Most notably, Greg credits his elder, Virginia Beavert, as a person who helps him see how crucial cultural revitalization is for Yakama peoples. Greg stated: "I just really wanted to work with the language, and a lot of that had to do with my elder, Tux̱ámshish Virginia Beavert." He told me that she serves as a strong role model for him, helping him see his calling to "do whatever I can to help." But working with Virginia was not Greg's first opportunity to learn from inspiring Native role models. Greg also credited other indigenous activists with inspiring him to form a nonprofit organization on the Yakama Reservation.

When I asked Greg how he got started working with the nonprofit organization X̱wayamamí Ishích, his response took us back to his teenage years, when he had just graduated from high school. He admits that, at that time, he had "no idea" what he would do with his life. He feels very grateful he had strong Native role models to guide him during this crucial time in his life. The strong role models he met would ingrain in him the importance of the Seven Generations philosophy. He reflected on how older activists inspired him as a young adult, which motivated him to carry on indigenous cultural revitalization work:

> I consider myself pretty lucky because when I graduated from high school I had no idea what I wanted to do, and [people would ask me], "Hey what are you going to do? You're supposed to know!" And I was like, "I don't know." And so I didn't really do a whole lot for a while. And then I got an opportunity to travel. I was a dancer, a fancy dancer for Native American powwows, and I met Binah McCloud, who was working for Chief Leschi [a Native American school operated by the Puyallup tribe in Western Washington]. She was organizing a Chief Leschi drum and dance tour, to go to Germany, Switzerland, and Austria. So I met her at a powwow and she's like, "Hey do you want to go to Europe with us?" And so that's how I got involved with that. And I liked it. And then I started getting real close with Binah McCloud, whose mom is Janet McCloud, who was an activist during the '70s who was a major part of the fishing rights struggle and she was a real amazing elder . . . Dennis Banks, one of the founders of the American Indian Movement, would come down to talk to Janet. And he came down once to do a run. And Binah called me and said, "Hey Dennis Banks is coming down to do a run, you should come out." So I came out and that's when I got the opportunity to meet Dennis Banks, who made a real good impression on my life. He was a real good leader, a real good person. He came in the community and he was making an Eagle Staff. And he said, "Hey, Greg, you know how to make an Eagle Staff?" And I said, "No." He said, "Come over here, I'll show you." And he just, you know, took a little time to get me started in what he was doing . . . And from then on I was traveling a lot with Dennis Banks. We did a run in Australia, New Zealand, then I went with him to Japan. We ran all over America, all across America a few times, all over. And I also was traveling with Chief Leschi, where I ended up getting a job, being a culture teacher there. And Dennis was like a role model for me . . . So Dennis had the Sacred Run foundation. And that's how come we were traveling everywhere. He had a nonprofit.

How it [Sacred Run foundation] got started was a whole bunch of elders got together in Canada to talk about all of the problems that were going on in Indian Country. The Cuyahoga River in Ohio was flammable from all these toxins in it. There were some trees in New York that were dying from the tops down because of the acid rain, and just all the problems going on everywhere and they were like, "What are we going to do?" And so they met, these elders, and they talked to each other for a few days. And then when they were done, they said, "All we can do is we can send out our message to people. They need to strengthen their ceremonies. We used to be ceremonial people. We need to strengthen our ceremonies. We need to go back to old ways of living healthier, being more in touch with Mother Earth. All life is sacred."

That was the main message. All life is sacred, and we just need to focus on that. Focus on ourselves and strengthen our ceremonies and remember that all life is sacred and respect the Earth. So Dennis thought, "Man, this is a real important message." You know, after all that meeting, all the stuff they could have done, for them to say that the Indian people across Indian Country need to strengthen their ceremonies and strengthen their old way of life, the way they used to eat, take care of themselves, and stuff like that. So, he thought, "Why just send this out in a press release?"

So he decided to revive an old tradition of sending runners from village to village with a message. So that's how the Sacred Run Foundation started, it started as a run going from one village to the next village, one tribe to the next tribe, and carrying this message, that all life is sacred, strengthen our ceremonies. And, that's how it started.

And from there it just grew and grew and I was lucky to be a part of it, and I got to travel a lot with Dennis all over the world, all over America, I spent a lot of time with them. And I learned all about him and his activities as an American Indian Movement leader. And I got to hear all the stories of all that type of stuff. I really, really was grateful to be a part of that. But, you know, I've seen him change a lot of lives. I've seen him go to Puyallup and work with the community in doing these runs, and he would take people like myself, young people, he'd be like "Hey, you ever tie an Eagle feather?" and that's all he would do with these young people, and we're talking like gangster-looking people you know. And they'd come over and talk with him and tie a feather or make a medicine pouch or something and they all end up having a lot of respect for him. And he changed a lot of lives. And I thought, all of this happened because of him doing this nonprofit.

Plus, when I traveled with Beena McCloud to Europe, that changed *my* life. And the people that went on it, I know that it changed their life, too, because they were all pretty young. We were all pretty young. I just turned eighteen and I was the oldest. Everybody else was just like fifteen, seventeen, or whatever. And you know from then on, they wanted to do better in their life, too.

So that is what made me think I want to do the same type of thing. I wanted to start an organization and I knew that when you know your language and your culture a little more, you have, you know, stronger self-identity and you know, just good stuff happens. So, anyways, all this stuff changed my life. It changed my life for the better and I was glad to be a part of it. So that's what I wanted to do in starting this nonprofit organization.

In his narrative, Greg discusses how his inspiration for co-founding X̱wayamamí Ishích reaches back to his youth, when he was doing cultural performances in Europe and becoming a culture teacher at a tribal high school. As a young adult, Greg was fortunate to be guided by strong women role models, Beena McCloud and Janet McCloud. Because of the women's encouragement, Greg had the opportunity to meet and work alongside Dennis Banks in a nonprofit organization that promoted indigenous social, cultural, political, and legal rights. Greg reflected on his journey and explained that those experiences "changed my life for the better . . . so that's what I wanted to do in starting this nonprofit organization." Quite simply, Greg wanted to found an organization to help the next generation of young people, so their lives could be better, and in turn could help build a more positive future for indigenous peoples. Greg's narrative serves as an example of what Sandy Grande describes as critical pedagogy, which connects politics to social responsibility and expands a sense of agency (Grande 2004). Greg learned, through participating in the dance group and organized runs, the basis of hope that underlies a critical indigenous pedagogy; in Grande's words, "a hope that lives in contingency with the past—one that trusts the beliefs and understandings of our ancestors as well as the power of traditional knowledge" (Grande 2004, 28). Greg learned from his elder mentor, Janet McCloud, that the main goal of working with youth is to teach them to "respect your own" community, which led to his idea of creating an organization on the

Yakama Reservation to help revitalize language and traditional cultural practices.

Greg discussed the importance of doing cultural revitalization work with children. In his comment, he mentioned how relationships across the generations are built into Yakama cultural teachings:

> I think the children have always been viewed as our future leaders. And you know, we are supposed to think of the seven generations ahead and the children are always important. In our language, Ichishkíin, there is the language that a granddaughter or grandchild will call their grandma, or grandpa. It is the same word back and forth. So my kids would call their grandma *Káła* and my mother in law would call her grandkids *Káła*, and talk about the special relationship that they used to have. And, the reason they had that special relationship is because a long time ago the adults would have to go out and gather food . . . and if you were an elder, you would just stay home and watch after the kids and it was more of your responsibility to help teach the kids. And teach them, tell them all of the legends and teach them all the stuff to help them grow to be a good person. And you know, the elders are leaving and a lot of people don't have very many elders in their family . . . the youth need a lot. There needs to be a lot more that they can do, you know? If they didn't want to get in trouble and run around on the street with a lot of these people, kids that might be doing that type of thing, you know, what are their choices? What else can they do? Because that's what kept me from doing a lot of that type of stuff, is because I met some good people who gave me a lot of guidance. And I think that's all they really need.

Greg's comments demonstrate the importance of intergenerational teaching and learning. He focuses on the special role of the grandmother and her grandchild, using the example *Káła* to illustrate his point about elders and children having a special relationship. This Yakama cultural teaching is a useful guide for Greg's work in revitalizing culture, as he seeks to help elders and youth become more meaningfully connected. Since westernization and assimilation have encroached upon the reservation, kinship relations, language use, traditional food practices, and other Yakama cultural traditions have been eroded. Thus, the work X̱wayamamí Ishích accomplishes is an important part of indigenous resistance to colonialism. Greg's comments clearly demonstrate how youth are central in revitalizing cultural traditions; however, he also shared how elders are critically important:

MJ: I've noticed in the nonprofit that elders are special teachers. Can you say a little about that?

GREG: We had a wind drying workshop and we probably could've found some people our age to do it, but there are some elders out there who have been doing this type of stuff for a long time, and you know, they know more than just how to wind-dry the salmon. They know stories about it. They can tell you about how it used to be a long time ago when everybody did it. And it is important to encourage these elders and give them the opportunity to come out and work with youth who want to learn these type of things. I know there are some elders who are happy when they get a chance to teach people these skills, and to teach the youth. I think that is real important to bridge the gap between the youth and the elders. And, so if there's something we're doing and there's an elder who is well-known for this type of work, then we would like to bring that person in, help them to teach the community and the youth, and I think it's important to involve the elders because they have the stories and the teachings.

Figure 5. Gutted Chinook salmon (donated by the Yakama Nation Fisheries Program) being taken to the youth so they can practice their new fillet skills at the X̱wayamamí Ishích workshop. (Photo by Michelle M. Jacob)

In Greg's narrative, we can see the importance of elders as teachers and role models. Elders are ideally situated to provide not only the technical skills but also the cultural teachings about traditional foods. In discussing his role as a X̲wayamamí Ishích co-founder, Greg credits his role models who mentored him as a youth. Such mentorship has a lasting effect not only in Greg's life, but in the community, as Greg now views community empowerment and cultural revitalization as his responsibilities. In his work with X̲wayamamí Ishích, Greg is instrumental in creating opportunities for his community to learn from the past and create a better future. By so doing, the people's cultural knowledge gaps are beginning to be filled. Young people learning the food traditions from elders helps to ensure that our people's relationship with our sacred foods remains alive. This is evidence of the power of the Seven Generations philosophy.

Women's Special Roles as Culture Bearers and Resisting Colonial Logics

One of the reasons that cultural knowledge gaps exist is the onslaught of colonialism and the pervasiveness of colonial logics within the US context. Greg's experience of being reawakened to the importance of cultural revitalization was linked to indigenous activism that resisted colonial logics of indigenous cultures as "dead" or "unimportant." Such logics render Native peoples as "vanished" and serve as a crucial tool for genocide and land appropriation, which further threatens the survival of indigenous peoples and cultural practices. Greg's mentors taught him ways of countering such logics through indigenous grassroots activism.

Within Native feminist scholarship, heteropatriarchy is a colonial logic identified as the building block of US empire. As Andrea Smith articulates, colonizers naturalized hierarchy by instituting patriarchy (Smith 2006). With the imposition of heterosexism and a rigid patriarchal order that assumes women as inferior to men, not only are traditional gender relations upset, but the very survival of indigenous cultural teachings becomes threatened, as the US capitalist empire marginalizes indigenous communities and epistemologies. Within the Yakama community, colonial patriarchy has upset traditional gender norms. Ackerman's study of Plateau Indian gender norms describes a social order of gender differences as "complementary but equal" (Ackerman 2000). My previous work provides evidence of early colonial encounters, with missionaries being distraught at how "haughty" Yakama women were, as they did not blindly submit to men's orders (Jacob and Peters 2011). Additionally, Yakama women have always been powerful economic agents, and previous work provides a discussion of how, historically, women controlled important sources of wealth and led successful labor disputes to ensure fair wages for their families (Jacob and Peters 2011). These examples of gender norms reinforce the "complementary but equal" framework that Ackerman uses and help illustrate a traditional Yakama horizontal form of power sharing. For example, within all important community tasks there is a gendered division of labor that respects men's and women's contributions equally. In the case of salmon fishing and preservation, men traditionally served as the fishermen who would catch the fish and then take it to the women, who would cut, preserve, and hold the fish supply. With the imposition of colonial heteropatriarchy, however, this Yakama social order has been upset, with cultural knowledge gaps erasing the practices of working with the fish, as well as the development of more hierarchical modes of leadership. Through their activist work, however, leaders within X̱wayamamí Ishích are resisting the colonial-imposed modes of leadership that denigrate or erase women's important contributions. This is a point I discuss further in chapter 4, when I analyze the theory-building contributions of Yakama decolonizing praxis.

In Greg's opening narrative, he discusses toxic pollution on indigenous lands as a common problem that led to a successful effort to mobilize resistance across several indigenous communities. The solutions proposed, according to Greg's recounting of the story: "We need to strengthen our ceremonies. We need to go back to old ways of living healthier, being more in touch with Mother Earth. All life is sacred." These solutions challenge the colonial logics within indigenous communities. "All life is sacred" refuses to institute hierarchy, as no living being is outside of the sacred realm. At the core of this principle is a profound respect for the feminine. Recognizing that indigenous peoples must restore balance and revive their traditions and ceremonies that connect them respectfully with the land—with Mother Earth—will help lead the people to a better place. Quite simply, indigenous peoples must return to traditions of having healthy lives that are centered on a respectful relationship with Mother Earth, who provides for the people. In this way, Mother Earth is a powerful representation of the feminine. As Sandy Grande has written, indigenous teachings understand nature as "a sovereign entity in symbiotic relationship with human subjectivity" (Grande 2004, 7). This indigenous-centered teaching undermines a colonial logic that imposes a human-nature hierarchy that situates humans as "masters" over nature.

Within the case studies of this book, women elders are repeatedly recognized as influential for their wisdom and patience as traditional cultural teachers. Greg's narrative demonstrates how he has internalized this teaching and, through his activist work, has a respect for affirming the importance of women as teachers. He recalls the powerful guidance women have provided for him and supports the importance of women as teachers. His attitude of affirming the importance of women's contributions situates women elders as powerful subjects. As such, the women elders resist the settler colonial hierarchy that would situate them as marginal—a "perpetual absence" in education systems and broader society (Smith 2010a). By contrast, women serve as strong and valued leaders within the grassroots efforts to revitalize culture within the work of X̱wayamamí Ishích. Other scholars have found a similar phenomenon among indigenous peoples, and indigenous women are often honored as culture bearers (Smith 2005a; Smith 2001). Some scholars link this to women's gifts of being nurturing, life-giving, and communally minded (LaDuke 2005b; Ackerman 1996). Indigenous women view culture-bearing as an honored responsibility, a point that is illustrated in Jessica's narrative below. Gender emerged as an important aspect of the cultural revitalization work that X̱wayamamí Ishích does within the Yakama community. The organization focused primarily on what are considered women's roles within traditional Plateau culture. Root gathering and drying, as well as processing meat and fish, are all considered women's activities and the source of women's economic power within traditional culture (Ackerman 1996, 12). Importantly, the elders who taught the traditional foods workshops were women. Although the success of X̱wayamamí Ishích workshops depend on traditional cultural contributions by men, such as the donation of fish for the salmon drying workshop, the actual task of fishing was not the focus of the food workshops, and thus men's roles were not prominently featured. Additionally, when I interviewed X̱wayamamí Ishích founders about the importance of women's leadership, they agreed that women, overwhelmingly, did the day-to-day busywork that kept the organization alive and well. Ranging from organizing workshops and gatherings, to managing paperwork, to applying for small grants and asking for donations, to caring for the children who attended X̱wayamamí Ishích activities, women indeed are the backbone of this volunteer organization.

In her interview, Jessica Sutterlict, a Winnebago/Santee woman who co-founded X̱wayamamí Ishích and serves as the organization's president, commented on the generosity of women who have worked with X̱wayamamí Ishích:

They have to be ready and willing to give their knowledge, like 100 percent. And we've been really lucky because the people that we have found so far are in their sixties, mid- to late sixties, and they are both women. These are the two that are doing the work, that did the workshops. The board is all women, except for Greg. We've talked about even working on the diversity on our board, to have more of a balance between men and women. But so far, it's harder to find men to take those leadership roles than it is women. Honestly, that personally is my own opinion. But also, I think, you know one of the things that you always hear, I've heard a lot of times, women are the backbone of the culture, women are the backbone of the society, all these things that make the strengths of the community. I do see that and I believe that. Even when you read other things about other

Figure 6. X̱wayamamí Ishích co-founder, Jessica Sutterlict, and her daughter. They are putting the smoked salmon into canning jars on the second day of a traditional foods workshop. (Photo by Michelle M. Jacob)

tribes, it talks about the culture is usually always passed down through the woman. So, it's a good thing. Even though I'm not Yakama, I still believe in the culture and that culture will definitely be passed down to my kids [who are Yakama]. And, too, a grassroots organization is really a nurturing process and it is very nurturing to the community and as women we have a nature of being more sensitive . . . I think we just have a better nature about, a passion of life. Especially when you have kids, you really understand what it's like to give up everything, your comfort and your life, for your kids. And so, it's easy to translate that into community, too, because when I think about it, when we're trying to nurture or contribute to the community, we're always contributing to our children because they *are* the community. And so when I think about it, when I'm old and I have grandkids and my grandkids are living in this community, what is the community going to be like for them? And so it's passing on your legacy or your hope for a strong community for your family and for other people's families, too, 'cause it has to be everyone working together to make a better place. But, yeah, I'm pretty sure the work part, like the paperwork, the organizing, the grant writing, all the little details of budget management, all that stuff is the women.

Women's dedicated role in carrying out the day-to-day work of X̱waya-mamí Ishích makes it possible to provide important cultural and educational opportunities for the community. Although fish drying and root gathering are traditionally women's activities within Plateau cultures, it is important to offer the traditional foods workshops to all community members, to fill persistent cultural knowledge gaps among Yakama peoples. None of the children or adults who attended the salmon drying workshop had ever practiced wind-drying fish, demonstrating the need for opportunities such as the X̱wayamamí Ishích workshop. When the women of X̱wayamamí Ishích provide this learning opportunity to their community, they empower both women and men because they are helping to fill a knowledge gap. Women's leadership in X̱wayamamí Ishích is consistent with what other scholars have found in their study of indigenous activism. For example, Linda Tuhiwai Smith discusses the role of women in the language revitalization activism taking place among Maori peoples. A strong result of their work is the Maori "language nests," which serve as indigenous language immersion educational sites for children and their families. Although the nests benefit and are supported by the community as a whole, it is the women who do the majority of the work to keep the nests alive and well (Smith 2001). Similarly, Andrea Smith found Native women were especially skilled and determined to engage in community-wide responses toward domestic violence in Native communities. Drawing from their collective vision of restorative justice, Native women activists refused to view domestic violence as an "individual problem" (Smith 2005a). Thus, I argue, the women of X̱wayamamí Ishích are carrying on a tradition of careful and nurturing collectivist work that is necessary to bring about change within indigenous communities. In this way, women are taking responsibility for their roles as culture bearers. Their hard work means the cultural teachings are surviving and benefiting another generation of young people on the reservation. While women sometimes lament that more men could assert a leadership role, especially with the busywork of day-to-day activities within cultural revitalization efforts, women's commitment to the collective well-being of the community overshadows any such critiques, a point that is further discussed in chapter 4. Perhaps, in the future, if X̱wayamamí Ishích chooses to focus on men's traditional cultural tasks (such as fishing or hunting), then men may emerge as stronger leaders in the day-to-day workings of the organization.

Ramona Kiona is the elder who is highly skilled at cutting and preserving fish and is featured in the ethnographic narrative at the beginning of this chapter. During our interview, she commented on her growth as a girl and young woman, when she made the decision to begin learning about working with the fish. Her comments help us understand how heteropatriarchy, as a colonial logic, serves to weaken indigenous cultural traditions. Her comments also help teach us the power of resisting heteropatriarchy to reclaim women's important positions within indigenous communities. When I asked Ramona where she learned about cutting fish, she responded:

> I learned from an eighty-some year old lady that was my grandmother's sister-in-law. And after I learned, it was just something that overwhelmed me that I wanted to do. Now when I was young I didn't even want to touch a fish. I was too young and beautiful to want to bother with a fish. It's a messy thing.

Ramona is recognized as an expert in fish cutting. She skillfully fillets and preserves fish, using old traditional methods such as wind-drying and smoking with wood chips, and newer methods such as canning and freezing. She describes the time when she learned how to work with salmon, noting an elder woman relative taught her. Ramona states working with the salmon was "something that overwhelmed" her. It was at that time she knew working with the fish would become very important in her life. This was a passion and dedication that developed for Ramona in adulthood. She notes that, as a young girl, she "didn't even want to touch a fish" because she felt that young, beautiful girls did not do such things, as it was "messy." Thus, Ramona had internalized the Western assimilationist teachings of girls needing to be "clean" and "away from dirty or messy things" and, assumedly, that girls should not be handling bloody knives or cutting out fish guts. These assumptions are mandated in heteropatriarchal logics of gender socialization that construct girls and women as in need of protection from all things "dirty" and "dangerous." For the younger generations of Yakama peoples, it is fortunate Ramona resisted such teachings when she entered adulthood, so she could become the precious elder teacher she is today. As such, she passes on teachings about food and culture that are under attack by the omnipresence of the Western junk food system, a school curriculum that fails to incorporate a Yakama health ecological view, and multiple other forces of assimilation that are perpetuated by contemporary settler colonialism. In figure 7, which builds upon Andrea Smith's theoretical work, I illustrate social and historical processes Yakama cultural revitalization efforts are resisting.

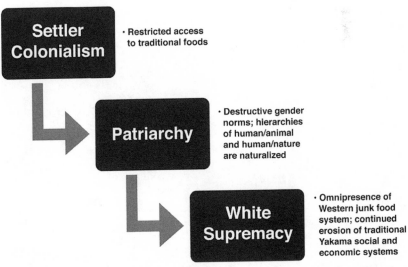

Figure 7. Contemporary challenges to Yakama cultural revitalization. (Drawing by Michelle M. Jacob and Christopher J. Andersen)

In observing her work with the children at the X̱wayamamí Ishích workshops, I noticed Ramona was exceptionally patient with the youth. She was generous in repeatedly explaining the different techniques children needed to use in order to cut the fish correctly. In my interview with Ramona, I asked her why she taught the food traditions and about her general approach in working with children:

MJ: Tell me why you wanted to do these workshops with the food and the younger people.

RAMONA: In working with the children you know the thing is that I treat people like I want to be treated. And I know it's their [the kids attending the X̱wayamamí Ishích workshop] first time [to work with fish]. I remember my first time. And [when I learned], the elder never yelled at me when I did fish. It's a culture thing. You cannot use harsh words over a food product in our culture. 'Cause whoever is going to eat that is probably going to get those vibes or they may get ill or something. If you look at our culture, if you're in one of our churches, and in the kitchen, if someone gets angry or sad, they need to leave the kitchen. Cooking and working with our foods, is an important attitude thing. And if we feel sad or mean or mad, we might as well just leave the kitchen because you are going to hurt somebody . . . if anybody is mean in the kitchen

Figure 8. Ramona teaches children how to fillet. (Photo by Michelle M. Jacob)

or sad, they're going to give those vibes [to other people] when they eat that food. And that's what our elders taught us.

Ramona's comments demonstrate how her work with X̱wayamamí Ishích is deeply spiritual. She feels it is important to teach food traditions to the youth. Ramona describes feeling "overwhelmed" with happiness in working with traditional foods, noting it was something she really wanted to carry on doing. She wants to share the food teachings and skills with youth, because she feels it will be a special gift to the children. Her teachings provide an important place-based education that nurtures the children. Ramona discusses cultural teachings about attitudes, feelings, and spirits when handling or even being around food. She shares that someone having an ill spirit around the food will inflict illness upon those who eat the food. She connects her kind and gentle teaching style to this cultural teaching, as she shares, "You cannot use harsh words" around the food. Thus, working with traditional foods is a deeply spiritual practice. The spirit and intent of the food preparers will affect the food itself, as the food will carry the spirit of those who touch it and pass it on to whoever consumes it. While Ramona's comments focus on the possible negative effects of this process, inherent in her teaching is also the message that food preparers must have a positive and gentle spirit while working with our traditional foods. Thus, a good spirit will be shared with the sacred foods (who have sacrificed themselves for the people), as well as the people who consume the food after it has been prepared. A main lesson is that spirits of people and our foods are interconnected. Ill feelings will be spread to others, so it is important to bring positive, kind feelings to share with others. By teaching the youth these important cultural lessons, the youth learn to respect the foods as sacred gifts, they respect each other, and, perhaps most importantly, they respect themselves as they realize their spirits matter and are interconnected with others.

Ramona provides an important teaching about a Yakama view of health ecology. Her comments demonstrate the interconnectedness of humans and non-humans, and that foods can transmit human energy and feeling from the food preparer to the person who eats the food. Ramona describes the importance of being patient when teaching youth about working with fish. She uses a gentle spirit and kind words to encourage the children as well as to pay respect to the fish and to the people who will eat the fish later. Ramona states in particular that sadness and anger, harsh words, and meanness around the food will in turn harm the people who eat it. Respecting foods as spiritual beings who can carry energy and intention is an important part of a Yakama health ecological view. Thus, the food system must be attentive to energy, reciprocity, and the profoundly complex set of relations that depend on food gathering, preparation, transport, and consumption. Having a system that, at any point, disrespects the foods or the peoples involved will bring illness to those involved in the food system. Humble and generous intention, attitude, and spirit must be central to all actions within the food system.

In order to ensure the survival of Yakama cultural teachings, these lessons, such as the ones Ramona provides about working with traditional foods, must be shared with the younger generations. The leaders of X̲wayamamí Ishích recognize this important point and look to women's leadership to carry out this important task. When I interviewed Greg about the future of Yakama cultural survival, he provided his advice for the future generations about learning cultural traditions. In his response, Greg identifies women elders as important culture bearers and teachers. He responded:

> We are at a scary stage, as Yakama people, our elders are getting older . . . It's very important to know who you are. There's a lot of elders out there who are willing to teach . . . these things that they know. So yeah, if you have an elder in your family, be thankful and talk to her . . . if you have one in your family definitely talk to her, and talk to him.

Greg's comments center on women elders. He instructs the future generations to be thankful for their elders, and he instructs them to "talk to her." Greg's comments support the importance of women elders as teachers, nurturers, and leaders in cultural revitalization efforts. Greg also adds at the end to "talk to him," as he recognizes men elders also have valuable teachings to share, but clearly, women are special leaders in the cultural revitalization work of X̲wayamamí Ishích.

Model of X̲wayamamí Ishích Work

I propose a model that guides the organization's cultural revitalization work. The model emerges through the activists' narratives. For example, Jessica's narrative shares the importance of intergenerational teaching and learning within a grassroots and spiritual context:

> So, yeah, there's always an emphasis on kids but the idea is also to have an exchange of knowledge between elders that are ready to pass on those skills and knowledge and ready to have that come to their

community and the people that are willing to receive it, whatever age group that is. It could be someone who is only five years younger than them, but if someone is willing to receive the cultural knowledge then that's the way it's going to continue . . . we've been blessed because Ramona is really busy. She actually takes care of all her grandkids and helps her son. So she is able to come on weekends. And the first time we worked with her, she showed up the day before, and she's a cute little grandma and is just so super sweet. And she helped us get stuff ready the night before 'cause we had no idea what we were doing. We got donations and just had no clue. And so she came and helped us. And then we got another contact of someone else. I believe that everything's meant for a purpose, especially things like that, so sacred and cultural, it's like those things that happen are, it's so good. It's meant to be that person. And those people that attend are meant to be there. And so I really have faith, I guess, and, I pray a lot that the person that comes into our life or into this program is a good person, is the right person. And it has been so far. So, that's how that's happened. So I don't know how it's going to be in the future but that's it so far.

As a co-founder of X̱wayamamí Ishích, Jessica approaches her activist work with a strong faith that the Creator will bring the right people into the work of the organization. Her work, then, is deeply spiritual, relying on the Creator to fulfill the mission of the organization. Additionally, Jessica's narrative teaches about the grassroots approach she takes, as she reaches out to the community for teachers and learners who are interested in revitalizing traditional cultural practices. This loosely structured way of working resists the formalities of a more institutionalized approach. It also allows a busy grandmother to assume the role of expert teacher, an unlikely result within a more formal setting.[1] Finally, Jessica's narrative shares the importance of intergenerational teaching and learning, which

---

[1] Jessica notes that Ramona is the caretaker for her grandchildren, a common role within Native communities. For example, according to US census data, 55.4 percent of American Indians living with their grandchildren assume caretaking responsibility, in comparison to 41.0 percent of the general US population's grandparents who live with their grandchildren, and 41.9 percent of white grandparents who live with their grandchildren. Native grandmothers are especially important in raising their grandchildren, with US census data indicating that 66.1 percent of American Indian grandparent caretakers are indeed grandmothers, in contrast with their white counterparts (59.2 percent) and the general US population (62.8 percent) (US Census Bureau 2010).

is the foundation of X̱wayamamí Ishích. The "exchange of knowledge" between an older community member and a younger community member is most important to X̱wayamamí Ishích. While oftentimes this means youth are learning from elders, it is also important to have younger adults learning from slightly older adults. This inclusivity is at the heart of the work X̱wayamamí Ishích accomplishes. No one is too young or too old to participate, as everyone is a valued participant.

Jessica, like the other activists interviewed in this book, also engages in her work with a great sense of humility. I asked her if she considered herself a cultural revitalization activist. She responded:

> I'm not the one revitalizing the culture. I'm not the one who has all this knowledge and stuff. The activists really are the people that are giving that knowledge. I just feel kind of like a facilitator. So, I facilitate other people being activists. I really don't know if I would call myself a cultural revitalization activist. But I think the community is, like the people that are facilitating, the people that are giving the knowledge, and the people that are receiving it, together are probably activists. I don't think you can separate it.

Jessica was quick to credit the people she works with as the activists, pointing out she herself did not carry the traditional cultural knowledge to be a revered teacher. She was humble in her response, only referring to herself as a "facilitator." Yet, in my participant observation with X̱wayamamí Ishích, I witnessed Jessica's skill in helping elders teach the workshops, as well as Jessica's generosity in assisting learners, of all ages, to attend the workshops and practice the new skills they learned. In so many ways, Jessica's activism makes the cultural revitalization work of X̱wayamamí Ishích possible, by opening up her home to host workshops, bringing people together, and securing the funds and donations necessary for the workshop materials. With her humble approach, she resists a colonial logic that would normally situate Jessica in a role of hierarchical power and importance, as president of X̱wayamamí Ishích. By refusing to uphold the hierarchy and instead taking a grassroots approach to making power by crediting "the people" and "the community" as the important activists and leaders, Jessica's involvement with X̱wayamamí Ishích challenges a colonial logic that naturalizes hierarchy to consolidate power among a few elites. She refuses to situate herself as the most important person or leader in the efforts of X̱wayamamí Ishích, and in doing so provides leadership centrally concerned with empowering those around her.

Figure 9. X̱wayamamí Ishích model. (Drawing by Michelle M. Jacob and Christopher J. Andersen)

My analysis of the activists' narratives has resulted in a list of the core values that underlie the work of X̱wayamamí Ishích, which I list below and have illustrated in a model that fits the spirit of the organization's work.

Values of the X̱wayamamí Ishích model:

Humility
Faith
Grassroots empowerment
Place-based teachings
Intergenerational teaching and learning

The values of X̱wayamamí Ishích are represented by the namesake of the organization, a beautiful golden eagle. The strong golden eagle serves as a protector over the precious place-based cultural teachings the organization seeks to preserve and revitalize through intergenerational teaching and learning. Humility and faith are the guiding values of the organization,

Figure 10. X̱wayamamí Ishích traditional foods workshop attendees. Note the wind-drying shed (on left) and two wooden smokehouses (in the middle and right) in the background, built by Jessica's father. (Photo by Christopher J. Andersen)

serving as the foundation of the eagle's wings. It is upon this approach to their work that X̱wayamamí Ishích activists have built their organization. At its heart, the model of X̱wayamamí Ishích holds a powerful message not only for those involved with the organization, but for all those who can make a contribution to healing social change by working toward a vision of education that upholds the ideals of humility, faith, and grassroots empowerment for intergenerational teaching and learning of place-based teachings.

Conclusion

As we have seen with other case studies in this book, grassroots activists view their work in spiritual terms. They view their work as a blessing upon themselves, and they wish to serve the community in a good way. Jessica noted she prayed to the Creator to ask for the right people to come into their lives, making the work of X̱wayamamí Ishích possible. She states that in every instance this has happened. She also believes the Creator is guiding their work; the Creator guides those who attend the workshops, so everyone there is "meant to be there." This trust, in the spiritual dimension of her work with X̱wayamamí Ishích, nurtures and sustains her through the difficult times of bureaucratic hassles, paperwork, and struggles to find enough funding and volunteers to keep the work going.

Despite these struggles, there is also an unwavering effort to keep work-ing toward the vision our ancestors held for us: to be a healthy community, rooted in traditional cultural teachings. When times become difficult, as inevitably they do for people working at the grassroots level, activists maintain their resistance by focusing on the promise of solving problems within our community by holding fast to our ancient traditions, following the Seven Generations philosophy, honoring women elders as culture bearers, and creating new methodologies to serve our people. Women serve as important leaders in this effort. As they reflect on their experi-ences, their narratives and actions are powerful examples that help dis-mantle colonial logics that naturalize hierarchy and further marginalize indigenous peoples and cultural practices. In their day-to-day work, the activists involved with X̱wayamamí Ishích are dedicated to resisting the patterns of assimilation that lead to cultural knowledge gaps for our young people. As with the other case studies in this book, the X̱wayamamí Ishích activists have the attitude of "just do it!" that tribal elder Virginia Beavert expressed in chapter 2. In the next chapter, we will engage the broader lessons activists shared regarding successes, challenges, and their hopes for the future. This vision, grounded in their tireless efforts to engage in activ-ism that brings about healing social change, serves as a theory of Yakama decolonizing praxis.

CHAPTER FOUR

Take Care of Your Past

Building a Theory of Yakama Decolonizing Praxis

Whip Man: An Ethnographic Introduction to Intergenerational Cultural Teachings

✳   ✳   ✳

The children stand still and quiet; they halt their usual squirming and chatter, demonstrating their focused discipline of stillness, attentiveness, and patience. They know what is expected of them, a result of the many hours of instruction they have received from elders and adults. The children's faces become serious as they wait to hear the elder's voice. After a long pause, a flute plays, loudly, beautifully; it is a suspenseful kind of noise. The children, dressed in their traditional regalia, remain still and focused, almost like statues. Then, after another pause, the elder's voice booms throughout the room. He is the Whip Man, a traditional figure in Yakama villages, who is responsible for disciplining the children.

The Whip Man's voice becomes the center of everyone's attention. He instructs the people about the importance of discipline, respect, culture, and community. The children, in unison, begin their sign language performance that honors the Whip Man's sacred teachings. The Whip Man is a special teacher who instills a strong sense of purpose and communal pride into the children. He knows that if the children learn these important lessons, then they will be strong individuals who ensure a strong community well into the future. He also knows that the children, often so present—and future-moment oriented, must be taught to respect the past, to learn from it, and to care for their ancestor's most sacred teachings. He repeats his strongest message several times, loudly, in his booming voice:

> *Take care of your past,*
> *Take care,*
> *You, you, you,*
> *Take care of your past.*

The instruction is firm, disciplined, but caring. One can hear the intensity in the elder's voice. The children embody his teachings as they point to their audience while the Whip Man states, "You, you, you. Take care of your past." In this way, the children are learning to be culture bearers. Through their performance they become teachers and messengers of Whip Man's traditional teachings.

*   *   *

Embodying Whip Man's Teachings and The Emergence of a Yakama Decolonizing Praxis

Children who performed the Whip Man routine with the Wapato Indian Club remember the basic teachings of responsibility and discipline that the elder's voice instructs. The poem, originally written by Phil George, was gifted to the Wapato Indian Club in 1989. The poem celebrates traditional figures (Whip Man and Whip Woman), who are responsible for disciplining children. Yakama elders Pauline Miller and Frank Gopher were so moved by the poem's message that they gifted background music and a vocal audio recording to the club, to be used in sign language performances (Wapato Indian Club 1994). The poem contains a powerful message that reminds young people to engage in an indigenous cultural practice of "heeding the voices of our ancestors" (Alfred 1995). In his interview, Haver Jim (whom readers met in chapter 1) talked about his memories as a participant in the Wapato Indian Club, and about needing to uphold the expectations of discipline and respect for the group. I asked if Sue's teachings about discipline had anything to do with his actions. He confirmed that it did. He agreed that club members needed to show discipline:

You had to. It is kind of a, living up to her expectations! You know she had a certain [way of expecting us to be], you had to have good grades, you had to show up to school every day. You had to behave yourself on the bus.

I asked Haver to say more about Sue's way of teaching discipline to the children. In his response, Haver reflects on why Sue was able to be strict yet still garner so much popularity and affection from the children. He points to her ability to communicate and positively reinforce the many good things children do, and an overall gentler style of discipline than what Haver had previously experienced:

I think it had a lot to do with her ability to communicate. Because of her training as a counselor, I know she did a lot of positive reinforcement. She was strict, but in a more modern way.

During his interview, Haver acknowledged that, as a child, he had a track record of discipline problems within the schools. Several teachers had written him off as perhaps a "lost cause," or at least a "troublemaker," who should be sent to the office and receive physical punishment, such as being hacked (a form of corporal punishment in which a student is hit with a stick) at school, for discipline problems. Despite this troubled record, Sue saw something more in Haver. She reached out to him and welcomed his participation and leadership in the Wapato Indian Club. She knew he had the potential to be a strong leader for our people. As Haver reflected on his experience in the public school system, and the importance of Sue's caring work with the children, he summed up his comments with perhaps the simplest statement that eloquently articulates the secret of working with middle-school children: "Sue treated me nice, so I behaved."

Haver's comments reveal the effectiveness of Sue's ability to teach discipline to children. Sue's work with the children demonstrates an approach to indigenous social change that I call Yakama decolonizing praxis. Sue draws from traditional teachings, such as Whip Man and Whip Woman, and uses new methodologies to share these traditions with the younger generations, such as helping children learn a sign language routine they can perform as part of the club's dance troupe. In this process, Sue teaches children they are precious to our people and have a responsibility to respect the past and build a positive future. My study of indigenous grassroots activism and the resulting theory of Yakama decolonizing praxis is a scholarly project centrally concerned with healing social change.

Defining Yakama Decolonizing Praxis

Throughout this book, I analyze examples of activism in order to articulate a theory of Yakama decolonizing praxis that advances our understanding of social change efforts concerned with "making power" to reclaim indigenous traditions, bodies, languages, and homelands. Through analyzing important case studies of "on-the-ground" activism, my study articulates the importance of drawing from traditional teachings and utilizing new methodologies, as activists work toward a vision of Yakama decolonizing praxis that: 1) understands indigenous bodies as sites of critical pedagogy, 2) centers social justice praxis to build a moral community, and 3) utilizes grassroots indigenous resistance as a mechanism to dismantle colonial logics.

Chapter 4 articulates how Yakama decolonizing praxis contributes to the growing body of work on theories of indigenous social change. The main theoretical camps I discuss are Native feminisms and radical indigenism/indigenous resurgence. These theoretical approaches share the goal of empowering Native communities and restoring Native cultural traditions. Despite these similarities, participants in theoretical work in these areas tend to lack detailed conversation with each other, which undercuts the ability of indigenous theories to make a greater impact in academic, policy, and grassroots arenas. This chapter emphasizes the importance of Yakama decolonizing praxis in order to weave a discussion across theoretical camps; by doing so, perhaps we can work toward more comprehensive, higher impact interdisciplinary indigenous theories of social change.

Native Feminisms

Yakama decolonizing praxis, which highlights the important place of women in cultural revitalization movements, builds upon Native feminist scholarship. Special issues of peer-reviewed journals (e.g., Goeman and Denetdale 2009; Smith and Kauanui 2008) have created valuable collections of essays on Native feminisms, and numerous scholars have contributed in this area (Maracle 1996; Ramirez 2008; Smith 2005b; Morgensen 2011; Mihesuah 2000; Suzack et al. 2010). The common theme across them, and what makes them inherently important as Native feminist texts, is the fact that each text centers Native women's experiences, utilizing gender inequality as a starting point for the analysis, and works toward envisioning a society in which our traditional cultural norms, which respect and honor women's contributions, are upheld.

Previous chapters in this book have detailed how the development of Yakama decolonizing praxis builds upon important contributions by Andrea Smith, Winona LaDuke, and Dian Million. Other scholars also help advance our understanding of the stakes of Native feminism. For example, Shari Huhndorf and Cheryl Suzack note in their essay about indigenous feminism, it "remains an important site of gender struggle that engages the crucial issues of cultural identity, nationalism, and decolonization particular to Indigenous contexts" (Huhndorf and Suzack 2010, 1–2). Huhndorf and Suzack articulate the need for critical indigenous feminist scholarship, noting our "common colonial history . . . transformed Indigenous societies by diminishing Indigenous women's power, status, and material circumstances" (3). In discussing the power dynamics involved in political projects, such as indigenous feminism, Huhndorf and Suzack note, "although Indigenous women must shape Indigenous feminism, Indigenous feminism—as a political strategy and project—also requires the alliances that are built through the engagement, contributions, and support of Indigenous men and non-Indigenous men and women" (4).

A central tenet of Yakama decolonizing praxis is that women are important as culture bearers and teachers. Women's leadership served as the "backbone" of cultural revitalization movements detailed in this book. The importance of women-centered movements is described by Rebecca Tsosie, who articulates women's leadership in Native communities as "an ethics of survival, of connection to the past generations, of responsiveness to needs of this and future generations . . . That spirit is what sustains Native peoples, what inspires us and gives us hope for the future" (Tsosie 2010, 29). Tsosie articulates Native women's leadership in terms of responsibility: "[I]n many traditions we are taught an ethic of responsibility in connection with our life's work. We are taught that the cycle of rebirth and regeneration that we all are part of places a great responsibility on us, to be appreciative, to remember what is important, and to serve our families and communities" (31). Tsosie further describes commonalities across Native cultures in her description of how Native women view themselves as connected to place and community: "Native women understood their existence as holistic—involving biological, social, and spiritual dimensions—and related through time and tradition to their lands, cultures, families, and communities" (31). Through her study of Native women's leadership, Tsosie articulates the following common patterns across Native cultures: "In most tribes, gender roles were perceived as complementary and not dichotomous" (32).

Across the case studies covered in earlier chapters, major lessons of Yakama decolonizing praxis are: the importance of Native women elders as culture bearers, the need to reshape educational institutions to serve our people, and the promise of grassroots activism for bringing about important forms of social change. Similar to the indigenous activists that Winona LaDuke (LaDuke 2005b; LaDuke and Alexander n.d.) and Andrea Smith (Smith 2005a) detail in their books, the activists I interviewed were motivated to engage in grassroots efforts in order to bring about social change that would benefit the younger generations. Thus, Yakama decolonizing praxis is centrally concerned with thinking intergenerationally. Activists were guided by the teachings and instructions of elders, and dedicated their lives to carrying out work that would benefit the future generations. Women are strong leaders in these efforts, providing evidence for both the need and the effectiveness of dismantling a heteropatriarchal colonial logic that relegates women generally, and women elders in particular, as marginal. These on-the-ground examples of Yakama decolonizing praxis make a contribution to existing theories that highlight the importance of gendered activism within indigenous communities. For example, Patsy (whom readers met in chapter 2), articulates an important aspect of Yakama decolonizing praxis, one which views women and men as equally important. I asked Patsy what motivated her to keep going in her work toward cultural revitalization. I noted her busy schedule working with the Northwest Indian Language Institute and other partners, as well as being active in national educational reform in her role as President Obama's appointee to the National Advisory Council on Indian Education (Ferolito 2010). She responded:

> I think what keeps me going, is the children but also the young adults that I work with . . . I always say to our children to be happy and to laugh, have a wonderful laugh whenever you can, because that is really healthy to have humor in our life. I just shared the other day with families that came together . . . and just to encourage our boys, in particular, to take the necessary steps for ensuring their own health at a very early age and not waiting until you get older. And this was all young men . . . often times with young men they feel like they need to be a macho person . . . and so one lesson is to take care of your health. Especially for the young men to take care of their health, too.

A main principle of Yakama decolonizing praxis is that our people are strongest when women and men work together to bring about healing for our people. While women I interviewed often acknowledged the special dedication and talent that women had for working collectively and taking care of day-to-day activities that kept grassroots movements going, they also acknowledged that this work would be incomplete without the support and involvement of men. For the men engaging in grassroots activism, they acknowledged the centrality of women, and women elders in particular, for providing them with necessary guidance and support, as they learned to embrace their leadership roles within community-based cultural revitalization activities. For example, Ryan (chapter 1) credited Sue with guiding him to embrace his culture and to see his potential as a performing artist. These are teachings he continues to draw on as a DJ for the tribal radio station and as a rap artist. In chapter 2, Roger discussed how his work to learn the language from Virginia taught him to be a better person, by internalizing teachings embedded within the language. He now shares these lessons with his own students. In chapter 3, Greg stated Binah and Janet McCloud helped him embrace the importance of cultural teachings at a time when he "had no clue" about what he would do with his life. Now in his work as a co-founder of Xwayamamí Ishích, he helps organize traditional foods workshops that honor women elders as teachers.

Across the examples of Yakama decolonizing praxis is an understanding that our people are healthy when we build movements with a gendered balance. This lesson is deeply rooted in traditional Yakama spirituality. The traditional longhouse teachings provide strict instruction in this regard, with women and men serving in particular roles, in particular spaces within the longhouse. Within the longhouse, there is a women's side and a men's side, and each side is respected as a sacred place. Lillian Ackerman has studied this gendered phenomenon among Plateau Indians, noting how traditional cultural practices are structured to provide a complementary gender balance of power and organization among our people (Ackerman 1996). Traditionally, everyday culture also holds a gendered division of labor among Yakama peoples. While men often fulfill the public leadership roles, they are only respected as leaders if they demonstrate an excellent ability to listen and provide for the people, with women serving as strong advisors. Leadership and generosity are expected of Yakama women and men alike. As Hunn notes in his study of Plateau Indian society, "generous men and women were often rewarded by recognition of their leadership potential" (Hunn, and Selam and Family 1990, 219). While Yakama decolonizing praxis will have the greatest potential when movements have a complementary gender balance, activists acknowledged our people are still working toward this ideal.

In examining the data from the three case studies, interviewees had strong opinions on the gendered dynamics of cultural revitalization movements. For example, Virginia questioned the economic and gender norms breaking down among Yakama people, and viewed this anomie as a threat to our cultural survival:

> I'm afraid the language is dying. And the culture is dying with it. What I see, I see people walking on the road and men just laying around out there in the shade in town and not working. Not doing anything! They're not all that old, you know. They are middle age, maybe even younger . . . And I don't know of what the future of this tribe will be. We need to put some self-esteem into our male people you know, that they need to look at what's happening to our tribe. Be more aware of it. It isn't all just per capita you know, there's a lot more involved to this tribe than just per capita. And I see all these addictions; that isn't part of our culture. I know that I'm not perfect, I can't, you know, point and say you know this is all wrong, but I'm just thinking I guess because I was raised the old way, that I faced a lot of hardships with my tribe, with my family, where I know that there are times when we didn't have enough money to do certain things, but you know we always had our cultural ways.

As an elder, Virginia remembers a time before settler colonialism had imposed such sweeping social change among Yakama people. For example, she recalls when families still relied upon gathering traditional foods as a main component of our economic order. These traditional ways featured a gendered social order where women and men assumed roles of importance. Now, with the imposed wage economy and restricted access to traditional foods and economic patterns, Virginia notes that men are often the people on the reservation who struggle to access and keep jobs. Her disappointment refers to the drug and alcoholism problems on the reservation, when she notes men "walking on the road" and "laying around in town." Virginia's critique of disrupted gender norms is confirmed by US census data, with single-woman–headed households overrepresented among American Indian families (21 percent) compared to the general population (12.6 percent), and the white population (9.6 percent) (US Census Bureau 2010). While these statistics can be interpreted in multiple ways, including pointing out the resilience of Native women to lead their households and raise families without the constant presence of a male, the statistics also provide a backdrop for elders' critiques, such as Virginia's, which acknowledge the need for a return to a healthy gender balance in leadership among our people. Single-woman–headed households are at particular risk for living in poverty. Within Yakima County, 17.2 percent of all families live below the poverty line, but 47.6 percent of female-headed households do so. Among female-headed households with children under five years old, 72.6 percent live below the poverty line, leaving women and children at a greater disadvantage with regard to a number of economic, educational, and health challenges (US Census Bureau 2012). Building a strong social movement to restore cultural traditions and to reestablish healthy gender norms are important potential outcomes for Yakama decolonizing praxis.

A concluding lesson, then, is that social change movements will benefit from a more complementary gender balance. Activists had some insight on how this could be accomplished, including: earlier and more in-depth prevention and treatment of addiction problems; greater economic opportunities for our people, especially for men; and, a growing need to return to our traditional cultural ways, including building our cultural activities into modern-day lifestyles. All of these solutions would help to restore men's and women's importance and responsibilities within our communities. As we work toward these solutions, we can see how grassroots efforts, such as founding the Wapato Indian Club, have already made a difference within the community. To help demonstrate this point, I will share an excerpt from Ryan's interview:

MJ: As you think about your educational experience, what impact do you think Wapato Indian Club had?

RYAN: It had a lot . . . discipline and behavior wise, because if I was going to be bad, and not listen in school, I wasn't going to get to go on that trip. Because if there is a trip going on, a kid wants to go . . . not only that, but the way Sue took a role, and you don't want to let down somebody that actually cares about your education. If there was some person [school official] that didn't act like they knew me, or just treated me like a stupid kid, or, back then they would say, "Oh wanna be gangster" or something like that. But I really wasn't, but that's what they would say. Well Sue wasn't like that. Sue would treat you like a family member would treat you. Sue would treat you like your own mother or grandmother would treat you, so you don't want to let down Sue! Sometimes you would of course, I mean you're a kid, you're thirteen, fourteen [years old], of course you're going to be doing stupid stuff. And Sue would tell you she's disappointed in you. But at the same time just to have her there at our school as a counselor made it so I wanted to get good grades. I didn't want to get in fights, or be doing stupid stuff, so, it was the Indian Club. Sue was the one that made Indian Club what it was, so, just having her there made it to where you wanted to do your best in school, to go on trips and to not disappoint her. So it impacted my education then. And then as I got older, the discipline that I learned from Indian Club carried over into high school to where I was trying so hard in middle school anyway and I had somebody that actually cared who was at the school in the middle school, I carried that over into the classes I had there.

Ryan's narrative helps us understand the implications of Sue's Yakama decolonizing praxis. Ryan states Sue's caring nature and high expectations helped him to become a better student and leader than he would have been if he had only interacted with school officials who assumed Ryan was a "wannabe gangster." Sue's message to Indian Club students such as Ryan was that the students were important and had great potential to contribute to our people's future. Yakama decolonizing praxis shares an empowering message that dreams of a better future for our people.

Patricia Penn Hilden and Leece M. Lee write about the importance of developing an indigenous feminist theory and articulate that theorists are dreamers, and indigenous feminist theorists are dreaming of a better future for our people (Hilden and Lee 2010). Yakama decolonizing praxis contains within it an activist call. Theory-building is useful only as it helps indigenous peoples to envision and work toward a stronger future. Sue's message to Ryan, and all the children who participate in the Wapato Indian Club, is that they are an important part of our dream for a better future for our people. This message is especially important for Indian boys, who are so often expected to die young, with lives full of violence, alcohol, and drugs. These stereotypes, rooted in tragic statistics that affirm the substance abuse problems and social ills within our community, are a legacy that grassroots cultural revitalization activists are working to undo. For every young person who escapes an early death, our people can mark another notable event in our collective history.

Time Ball, History, and Social Change

Yakama decolonizing praxis draws from the place-based teachings of Yakama cultural practices. Across the case studies, activists emphasized the importance of place and history. Our people have a strong tradition of being historians. According to our people's traditions, women are central in documenting important events, happenings, and memories for our people. This tradition is evident in the phenomenon of the time ball. The Yakama Indian Nation Cultural Center describes the time ball in the following way: "Time is a relationship between events, Kept fresh in memory by selected objects on knotted hemp. Connection is as vital as Separation. The strand is begun by a woman at her marriage. By the time she is a grandmother, The unity of life is wrapped and remembered in a Time Ball" (Uebelacker 1984, 10).[1]

This book has been an effort to help mark and record this historical moment of important activism and grassroots organizing taking place on and around the Yakama Reservation. Like all efforts to create a time ball, this book cannot tell all stories for all times. But it does provide an important "partial perspective" of the work that is being done to reclaim our traditions, empower our people, and articulate a Yakama decolonizing praxis that will benefit the future generations. In that vein, this book represents both Native feminist as well as radical indigenist work. In the next section, I turn to a discussion of radical indigenism and indigenous resurgence, analyze the central tenets of this area of indigenous studies, and offer thoughts on how Yakama decolonizing praxis contributes to that broader discussion.

Radical Indigenism and Indigenous Resurgence

Yakama decolonizing praxis is rooted in a political commitment to social change that draws upon indigenous culture and identity, and thus builds upon theories of radical indigenism and indigenous resurgence. Broadly speaking, the theorists in these areas work in the social sciences, including sociology and political science. Of special note is Eva Garroutte's (2003) theory of radical indigenism, and Taiaiake Alfred's (2005) theory of indigenous resurgence. What these theorists share in common is that they articulate an activist call based on the belief that tribal peoples are best situated to reclaim our traditions, identify our most pressing needs and problems, and build solutions to our own problems, based on traditional teachings.

---

[1] See the following link to view a photo of a Plateau Indian holding a time ball, from the Yakima Valley Regional Library Relander Collection: http://www.yakimamemory .org/relander/image/1319.jpg.

At the heart of these theories is a dedication to reclaiming one's indigenous traditions. Strong individual tribal people are collectivist-oriented, yet feel an individual sense of responsibility to work toward the collective good. As such, these theories are inherently concerned with applied examples and scholarship. Theoretical work is important only to the extent that it makes sense, and matters, on the ground—the grassroots level on which indigenous peoples are working.

Eva Garroutte's theory of Radical Indigenism, for example, which is primarily concerned with American Indian identity, resists what many indigenous peoples view as the pitfall to Western scholars' theoretical work on identity, the so-called navel gazing that asks abstract questions about identity that are not rooted in a critical historical understanding nor connected to contemporary tribal needs. Garroutte engages complex and emotionally charged issues in a way that simultaneously educates and advocates for American Indian community empowerment. For example, Garroutte draws from multiple forms of data in order to analyze the many complications surrounding American Indian identity. Ranging from racial and biological notions of blood quantum, to the meaning of indigenous language use and loss, to stereotypes that are deeply embedded in US popular culture and the media, Garroutte's analyses help us understand the many ways in which American Indians must negotiate seemingly endless complications surrounding our identities. Garroutte reveals the link between identity and epistemologies and calls for a *distinctly American Indian scholarship* that makes the academy a "safe place for indigenous knowledge." Her major contribution, then, is the development of the theory of Radical Indigenism, which argues for the "reassertion and rebuilding of traditional knowledge from its roots, its fundamental principles" (Garroutte 2003, 101). Garroutte explains that a new, American Indian scholarship must be *spiritual* at its core. In her words, "Radical Indigenism suggests resistance to the pressure upon indigenous scholars to participate in academic discourses that strip Native intellectual traditions of their spiritual and sacred elements" (103–104). This theoretical approach has methodological implications, and the "twin requirements of Radical Indigenism" are 1) researchers must enter tribal philosophies, and 2) researchers must enter tribal relations (110). This ensures that Native spiritualities, philosophies, and community empowerment are at the heart of scholarly endeavors. Thus, Garroutte's vision of a Radical Indigenist scholarly project is one that subverts the old colonial power relations that dispossess Native peoples of our lands, cultures, identities, and humanity. It is a vision that reclaims the centrality of our spiritual and cultural traditions and relations of kinship.

My work in articulating a Yakama decolonizing praxis builds upon Garroutte's theory of radical indigenism. Across the case studies that we have examined in this book, activists engaged in a diverse array of work. Yet, common across the cases is a commitment to doing work that revitalizes traditional Yakama culture. Activists think creatively and work both within, and without, mainstream institutional support. Accordingly, they vary activities and strategies, but constant within their work is a dedication to carry out their elders' instructions to help the people. They view their work in spiritual terms, and they credit their work with helping them to become better people, evidence that their cultural revitalization work nourishes their spirits. Staunchly committed to an intergenerational approach to teaching and learning, activists are quick to acknowledge that their elders are the wisdom keepers, and that it is the duty of the younger generations to learn and share the Yakama place-based teachings that will empower our people, protect us from social ills, and build community.

Theorizing the Politics of Yakama Decolonizing Praxis

Most interviewees were hesitant to embrace the labels "feminist" or "activist." They also resisted framing their work in explicitly political terms, although they were aware of the implicit political complications of doing cultural revitalization work. For example, Wapato Indian Club founder, Sue Rigdon, noted in her interview that some community members critiqued the young dancers for "not doing the dances right." Sue rarely challenged such criticisms publicly, but in private she would remind youth that there was more than one way of doing the Welcome Dance hand gestures, for example, and that depending on where an elder was from, they might have a slightly different way of rotating their wrist and moving their hands. But, Wapato Indian Club dancers were doing the version of the Welcome Dance "correctly" in accordance with the teachings that Sue and other elders had gifted to the youth.

Additionally, adults and youth who attended the X̱wayamamí Ishích salmon drying workshop shared that they had elders or adults in their lives who doubted their abilities to learn the food traditions successfully. For example, Ramona recalled that, during her childhood, some adults sternly refused to let children touch salmon, telling the children that they would "ruin" the fish with sloppy cleaning or fillet techniques. Ramona reflected on this experience and understood the adults' perspective, because of the high value of the salmon. However, she also knew that today's youth oftentimes are simply less likely to be around fish, as their families usually depend on a Western, assimilated diet. Children are unlikely to learn how to cut fish if they have never even touched a raw fish, as was the case with nearly all of the children attending the X̱wayamamí Ishích workshop that Ramona taught. At the workshop, when children mistakenly cut off salmon tails, Ramona had a choice to scold the child for doing the task incorrectly, or she could gently redirect the children, patiently showing them by example and using repetition to teach the necessary skills. Ramona chose to do the latter, reminding children "This is the way I was taught. If you have an elder who prefers to fillet a different way, then listen to them, but today this is how we should try to do it." With such a gentle teaching approach, Ramona redefined the role of children in learning traditional food practices. Rather than sternly telling them "they didn't know how to do things," Ramona felt it was appropriate to teach the children with patience, repetition, and with a humble attitude that her way was not necessarily the only correct way to handle fish.

This example illustrates the political battles over who knows the "real" cultural traditions and the contentious ground upon which indigenous activists and our allies must walk. Taiaiake Alfred writes about these issues in his book, *Wasáse*, noting that indigenous peoples can sometimes lose sight of our ultimate goals, and in doing so, derail our own efforts to build a social movement that protects our people and cultures (Alfred 2005). For example, in urging that indigenous peoples keep in mind the need to work toward "spiritual-cultural resurgences," Alfred also recognizes that not all indigenous peoples are uniformly concerned with taking action to resist colonialism, stating, "Many people are paralyzed by fear or idled by complacency and will sit passively and watch destruction consume our people. But the words in this book are for those of us who prefer a dangerous dignity to safe self-preservation" (24). Thus, Alfred acknowledges that there are a diversity of perspectives and political attitudes within Indian Country. Not all people will be interested in indigenous resurgence movements, nor will they be supportive at all times. Sue's comments about children being critiqued in their attempts to learn traditional dances is an example of this. Some children are rebuked so heavily that it seems as if some adults would prefer the children to assimilate, forgetting or ignoring their connections to tribal cultural traditions. But in continuing to work against such negativity, Sue helped to build a positive opportunity for children to learn or relearn some of their tribal traditions. In this way, the Wapato Indian Club provides an example of dangerous dignity within the community.

My articulation of Yakama decolonizing praxis helps extend the work of indigenous resurgence scholarship by providing details of place-based teachings and grassroots movement activities, challenges, and motivation. By studying the work taking place in the Wapato Indian Club, the partnership with the Northwest Indian Language Institute, and X̱wayamamí Ishích, we learn how everyday people are seeking to transform our institutions to better serve our people. At the heart of all of the activist work that I examined in the case studies, there is a recognition of the timeliness of this work—as our people realize how precious and limited our time is with our tribal elders, who hold the traditional teachings and histories of our people. It is up to the younger generations to reach out and learn the teachings, to create educational environments and alternative structures in which we can pass the teachings down through the generations, and to build a broader social movement in which all peoples are empowered to reclaim our culture, education, and health as individuals and a stronger collective. In this way, Yakama decolonizing praxis supports and extends the important theoretical work being done in the area of indigenous resurgence.

Yakama Decolonizing Praxis and Human Rights

To conclude this chapter, I situate Yakama decolonizing praxis in the broader discussion of indigenous peoples' rights and social change. Indigenous communities face numerous social problems, rooted in the legacy of colonialism and manifested as contemporary soul wounds. The case studies within this book, which inform the articulation of Yakama decolonizing praxis, demonstrate the importance of grassroots cultural revitalization efforts taking place on and around the Yakama Reservation. The lessons learned from the case studies contribute to the growing body of work on indigenous social change. Two ways that existing literatures can be brought together are through a focus on future generations and the protection of indigenous human rights. Activists can heed the voices of their ancestors and protect our peoples' rights to culture and health through various ways, including: teaching youth traditional dances, reinforcing the message that educational persistence matters, learning to speak and understand their indigenous language, and teaching youth how to engage in traditional food ways. The models provided at the end of each case study (chapters 1, 2, and 3) can inform other communities as they begin or persist in their own place-based decolonizing praxis.

Important international documents, such as the United Nations Declaration on Human Rights and the United Nations Declaration on the Rights of Indigenous Peoples, articulate that indigenous peoples have the right to learn and use their languages as a basic human right. Tove Skutnabb-Kangas and Robert Dunbar (2010), scholars of indigenous human rights, argue that resisting "subtractive" forms of education (such as English-only policies) benefits all peoples. In their work, Skutnabb-Kangas and Dunbar draw from global examples of indigenous community members and grassroots organizing to establish the importance of cultural and linguistic rights. For example, within their work, they cite Ofelia Zepeda, a Tohono O'odham linguist, who explains "language is the gift from the Creator" and refer to the Resolution No. 9/90 Protection of First Nations' Languages, from the Special Chiefs Assembly in Canada, which states, "First Nations languages are the cornerstone of who we are as a people . . . our culture cannot survive without our languages" (Skutnabb-Kangas and Dunbar 2010, 37). Such examples clarify that indigenous peoples view language survival as directly related to the cultural and spiritual health of our people.

In the Northwest Indian Language Institute case study in this book (see chapter 2), Yakama Reservation community members articulate language loss as one of the highest priority needs within our community. In the words of our elder, Virginia Beavert, "I don't want the language to die!" Yakama decolonizing praxis teaches us we are at a critical point in time in our people's history, but our people have the capacity and the determination to resist neocolonial patterns of subjugation. A culturally relevant image that we can return to, then, is the time ball. Collectively, we can begin making a knot in our people's time ball, to mark this important point in history, when we bravely stand and look at the proud past of our people, and the ways in which we can work together to bring about a healthy, vibrant future for our people. I contend that as we continue to work, and develop our theory and praxis, we will indeed bring about a great healing among our people. In chapter 5, I draw from Yakama decolonizing praxis to articulate a set of recommendations that can serve as a next step toward healing social change.

CHAPTER FIVE

The Renaissance Is Now

Next Steps for Healing and Social Change

This book has focused on cultural revitalization efforts particular to the Yakama Reservation community. However, lessons learned through these case studies can be helpful for other peoples who are interested in developing indigenous-centered educational models that bring about healing social change. As stated in the Introduction, all peoples who live, work, learn, and play on indigenous homelands have inherited the legacy of colonialism. In order to heal the soul wounds of intergenerational historical trauma, all peoples have an important role to fulfill. We all benefit from healing social change. The title of this chapter is inspired by Yakama elder, Sue Rigdon, whom readers met in chapter 1. During our interview, Sue shared her message about indigenous cultural revitalization. It was simple and optimistic; Sue said, "The renaissance is now."

Building upon the spirit of Sue's message, this last chapter serves as an activist call for greater support of grassroots indigenous cultural revitalization. Here I briefly discuss the important connections between activist scholarship and cultural revitalization efforts that can help advance the mission of decolonization within indigenous studies. As articulated in the Introduction, the definition of decolonization I use constructs indigenous peoples' efforts to reclaim traditional cultural practices as a foundational approach to recognizing and addressing the legacy of colonialism within our communities. Because Western institutions rarely acknowledge or support such cultural revitalization efforts, grassroots activism and activist scholarship are two approaches that have proven useful in the case studies analyzed within this book, and have a broader lesson that can be applied in other settings. The recommendations that conclude this chapter serve as a contribution to the ongoing discussion of *how* we can engage in activist scholarship that advances decolonization efforts. Inherent in my call for activist scholarship is an awareness of the resources that Western educational institutions *can* provide to help support indigenous-led cultural revitalization efforts. Since decolonization is about empowering indigenous communities, I propose recommendations that work toward a model of activist scholarship that supports community members and academics.

Indigenous Activist Scholarship

The applied vision I offer here is rooted in a tradition of indigenous studies that seeks, above all else, to produce scholarship that is relevant for indigenous communities. For example, Devon Mihesuah articulates the ways in which an indigenous scholar can use scholarship to serve the community. Mihesuah states: "I feel strong emotional pulls in numerous directions: to my homeland and family that are the foundations of my identity and to my job, where I can accomplish much in the way of dispelling stereotypes and educating Native students so they can become effective catalysts who will ensure their tribes' survival. I am an activist" (Mihesuah 2003, xxi). Other indigenous studies scholars share a similar vision, such as Taiaiake Alfred, who recognizes the importance of indigenous academics having humility, as he models with the statement, "I do not pretend to any higher wisdom on Mohawk culture or tradition. My intended contribution, and my aspiration, is to present a view firmly rooted in a Native world and solidly grounded in the scholarly world. As one who is fortunate enough to walk in both, I take it as my responsibility to create bridges between the two worlds that others may use to heal the rifts that have developed between us" (Alfred 1995, 1). Finally, activist scholarship that envisions healing social change is especially important for those of us who work within indigenous studies. Eva Garroutte poses the question, "What does it mean for me and other Indian scholars to live out our responsibilities to our cultures and our people in the academy?" (Garroutte 2003, 143). As indigenous scholars, it is our task to reclaim the stories and traditions of our people. Such cultural work nurtures our people, both the generations past, as we honor them, and the future generations, as we seek to carry out elders' teachings for the future generations' benefit. We have a responsibility to go about, to the best of our abilities, doing this nurturing work.

Such a vision is also inherently optimistic, as it works toward building positive solutions to problems, rather than staying focused on the negativity of the many problems within our communities. In using this approach, I am following the example of the activists whom I had the honor of interviewing and observing within my home community. The activists I interviewed acknowledged the difficulties that our people face in terms of recovering and revitalizing our cultural traditions, yet they also were optimistic about our future as a people. They believed their work made a difference and, in conducting my field research, I witnessed the difference it made within the activists' lives, as well as in the countless lives they touched through their grassroots educational activities. Their efforts are part of a larger social movement to reclaim our bodies, cultural practices, foods, and educational institutions. It is a movement that works toward a healthier future for our people, relatives, and our homeland. This optimism has emerged out of a painful colonizing past. Gloria Bird, a Spokane writer, discusses the optimism involved in cultural revitalization efforts:

> Native people's stories, histories, very beings are inheritors all of a legacy of pain and disinheritance, but to speak of colonization only in those terms is to stay within the realm of creating boundaries between *us* and *them*, to stay locked into a static system with no resolution—that can in fact subvert the healing/shift that is necessary in the process of decolonization. In using the language of the oppressed, we repeat the same patterns of our initial siege . . . we are perpetuating notions of our own inferiority and domination. In order to move out of the colonizing instances of interiorized oppression, we first must identify those moments in which we reinforce those useless paradigms and search for new approaches to the way we speak of ourselves in relation to our histories and stories. To imagine a future. (Bird 2005, 103)

Bird urges indigenous peoples to create a future that transcends colonial constructs and instead defines ourselves and our communities from a decolonized perspective. Such a vision depends on a deep commitment to the collective good, as indigenous peoples oftentimes must make great sacrifices to reclaim traditional knowledge and cultural practices. However, with a strong sense of purpose, activists can be successful in revitalizing cultural traditions. Their leadership can be a powerful "secret weapon" in building a healthy future for our people (Cornell et al. 2007).

The activists I interviewed are busily creating that new future for our people, out of a deep concern for the well-being of tribal youth. For example, in the front matter of the comprehensive Yakama dictionary, Virginia Beavert, whom readers met in chapter 2, writes:

> My message to the Yakama people is that learning to read and write your own language is very important. It is the only way to save your native language and culture for the future generation. We are losing our elders every day as they depart to a better place. My purpose in developing this dictionary has not been to benefit myself, but to encourage the younger generation to pursue an education, learn the language, teach their children to speak, read and write Sahaptin, and do their part to help preserve the native language and culture of the Sahaptin people. (Beavert and Hargus 2009, xvii)

Beavert uses her own scholarly work to convey an activist call for community members to embrace education to help the future generations. The special focus on youth is a common theme across indigenous political movements—as indigenous peoples seek to bring about social justice for the purposes of protecting the future generations. All of the activists I interviewed acknowledged that they persisted in their work so that the future generations could benefit. The struggle for liberation was never *only* for the present generation, but to ensure a lasting intergenerational impact that would ultimately help to restore healthy indigenous communities. Indigenous youth were often specifically mentioned as a primary motivator for young adults and elders involved in social change efforts, as activists worried whether the youth would have knowledge of their tribal language, traditional foods, and dances. Cultural revitalization efforts must place a special emphasis on reaching out and working with young people, an argument that Minnie Grey also proposes in her discussion about Inuit women and politics:

> Our youth are our future, and we need their involvement. I know that life can be a struggle, especially in trying to find a place and an identity, but be optimistic and know that things have a way of turning out for the better. Our youth need to take advantage of the best of both worlds, as my mother taught me and as I continue to strive to do today. (Grey 2010, 28)

Activists that I interviewed embraced the vision Virginia Beavert and Minnie Grey articulate. The sense of using the best tools from both (indigenous and Western) worlds allowed activists to draw from the teachings of their elders and create new methodologies for change. Activists engaged in what I call Yakama decolonizing praxis were creative in their partnership-building with educational institutions (working with the Wapato Middle School to create a dance troupe), with other nonprofit organizations (obtaining funding from Honor the Earth to support traditional foods workshops), and through the use of media (websites, Facebook, and distributing CDs that contain language lessons and recordings of elder speakers) as a way to do educational outreach.

The Spiritual Roots of Indigenous Activist Scholarship

Across the case studies featured in this book was the acknowledgement that cultural revitalization work is spiritual. Activists felt "blessed" to be involved with their work to learn and teach dance, language, and food traditions. Other indigenous scholars also emphasize this theme. Mililani Trask reflects on the ways in which she views Native activism as spiritually based: "What I learned when I became involved in political issues is that our perceptions as women very much relate to our cultural, racial, traditional backgrounds. I found that my work, which is primarily political work, became spiritual work as well" (Mihesuah 2003, 143). Janice Gould describes how indigenous peoples' belief in the Seven Generations prophecy is a spiritual vision that teaches intergenerational responsibility. Her description complements those that activists provided within our featured case studies:

> "We cast our prayers seven generations ahead." Many Native people say this. Also we say that we listen to the ancestors, so we cast our prayers seven generations behind, too, as we try to hear the memories that come before the individual memories we believe are our own. We are, of course, someone's seventh generation. Back in the spiral of time, somebody prayed for us and hoped we would listen and hear. Our stories create our world. The heart's responsibility in all this is to hear, hold, and translate the stories it receives from memory and from the small beautiful objects of our world that probably never come to the attention of the rational, cognitive mind. (Gould 2005, 11)

Gould's imagery of the heart's responsibility provides direct instruction: listen, remember, share (or, in her words "hear, hold, and translate the stories"). Gould's message about the interconnectedness of the generations reminds us of how we are responsible for others' well-being.

Indigenous activists that I interviewed engaged in cultural revitalization work out of concern for their community. Community needs drove their actions and inspired their hopes for a better future. Their work, and the models that underlie it, have much to offer for readers who are concerned with social change, healing, and culture. We have much to learn from people who are working "on the ground" out of a motivation for change that was sparked by the instructions of a tribal elder. As such, the case studies within this book, and the overall book project itself, has attempted to be an example of what Eva Garroutte has termed *Radical Indigenism*, a theoretical perspective discussed in chapter 4 and defined as "a scholarship in which questions are allowed to unfold within values, goals, categories of thought, and models of inquiry that are embedded in the philosophies of knowledge generated by Indian people, rather than in ones imposed upon them" (Garroutte 2003, 144). For example, a common approach used in all three case studies was focusing on youth as important learners of traditional teachings. The intergenerational approach to teaching and learning was a guiding philosophy as well as a methodology that activists applied. Patsy Whitefoot, the past president of the National Indian Education Association, whom readers met in chapter 2, discussed this approach in terms of "the principles of the value that we hold for Native children . . . looking at the whole child." In her leadership role, Patsy helped to draft a policy statement called the Native Children's Agenda, which holds these values as central for all Indian education work. The Native Children's Agenda attempts to influence self-determination policy in ways that go beyond simply calling for another report (Castile 2006). As someone involved in Indian education at the national level, Patsy travels to Washington, DC, where she navigates committees, hearings, and briefings to remind policy makers of the importance of protecting indigenous cultures. She uses her grassroots approach to articulate the message that taking action to support culture and language revitalization is crucial for improving our people's education and health. At the center of her work is a belief that policy is active; it is a verb (McCarty 2011).

The focus on applied work is intentional, as it benefits indigenous communities directly, often serving as a source of empowerment. Devon Mihesuah discusses the ways in which activism and cultural expression can empower Native peoples. She writes, "For many Natives dancing is not just an expression of identity; it is also a form of worship, healing, and celebration. Teaching one's children to dance assures the continuation of tribal culture and kinship ties, and attending powwows, stomps, and other dances is one way to socialize and celebrate community" (Mihesuah 2003, 154). She mentions the Nuvatukayaovi Hopi Youth Dance Group, who share a similar vision to the Wapato Indian Club, in that self-esteem, cultural pride, and intergenerational teaching are emphasized within the group. It is important to situate scholarly discussions about cultural revitalization within the local, grounded context of contemporary indigenous communities. Theory-building that is attentive to, and responsible to, contemporary Native communities has a much greater potential to interrupt systems of inequality and make a contribution toward "emancipatory possibilities" (McCarty 2011).

Recommendations

To conclude this chapter, I share recommendations for next steps forward in this journey. I hope other indigenous communities and educational institutions can apply these recommendations within their own contexts. I began this chapter by drawing from Sue Rigdon's words that explain the contemporary moment as being one of renewal and hope. As an elder, Sue reflects on our people's past and remembers all the struggles that we have encountered. She realizes our people continue to struggle in many ways, but that today is different. She believes the current generation is the prophesized healing seventh generation. Her conclusion is, "The renaissance is now." With those words, I hope all readers are encouraged to envision their roles as activists in the journey toward healing social change. As readers of this text, I hope that you take up the activists' call to build the movements.

If you are a member of a university community, here are specific recommendations you can help achieve within the university:

1. Recognizing formally the importance of respectful partnerships with tribal communities
2. Dedicating staff, faculty, programmatic, and curricular resources to outreach, implementation, and maintenance of tribal partnership relationships, including visiting tribal peoples on their home reservations
3. Committing to ongoing involvement and visible support for the partnership from all levels (student, staff, faculty, administration) of the university

4. Sharing power with tribal partners, with the focus on applied and relevant knowledge production that benefits tribal communities
5. Hiring and supporting culturally competent university personnel who have the authority and autonomy to be flexible in their efforts to plan, implement, and lead tribal partnership work

If you are a member of a tribal community, here are specific recommendations you can work toward in grassroots efforts and within formal tribal programs:

1. Conducting ongoing outreach efforts to educational institutions that may be beneficial partners
2. Identifying and supporting tribal community members who have relevant knowledge and skills to help build educational partnerships
3. Recognizing the constraints (budget, assessment, lack of authority) placed upon personnel within educational institutions and being willing to help work around such constraints
4. Being clear on the priority needs within tribal communities
5. Supporting (philosophically, emotionally, financially) tribal members who serve as a "bridge" between tribal communities and universities

These recommendations represent practical ways in which various bodies may better implement and support indigenous cultural revitalization efforts. This vision, articulated so well by the activists I interviewed, serves as the basis for important forms of healing social change taking place on the Yakama Reservation. The vision privileges an activist scholarship and centers a decolonizing agenda. The case studies detailed in this book teach us that our traditional cultural teachings really do hold within them the answers to our peoples' problems. This book has detailed grassroots processes and models, which I call a Yakama decolonizing praxis, that are making a difference in peoples' lives. I thank all the participants for their generosity in sharing their experiences so they could help teach me, as well as you, the reader. Now that you have been gifted with these stories we hope you will, in turn, offer up your own gifts to help build movements that promote finding ways to listen to our elders, working collectively, and reaching out to others who can join these movements and help make them bigger and better.

Appendix

Interview Guide
Cultural Revitalization Discussion Topics
1. Years involved
2. Why participation is important
3. Favorite memory
4. Teachings taking place
5. Children and cultural pride
6. Impact of involvement on life
7. Message for future generations

References

Ackerman, Lillian A. 2000. "Complementary but Equal: Gender Status in the Plateau." In *Women and Power in Native North America*, edited by Laura F. Klein and Lillian A. Ackerman. Norman: University of Oklahoma Press.

———. 1996. *A Song to the Creator: Traditional Arts of Native American Women of the Plateau*. Norman: University of Oklahoma Press.

Advocates for Indigenous California Language Survival. 2012. Accessed November 17, 2012. Available from http://www.aicls.org/.

Alfred, Gerald R. 1995. *Heeding the Voices of Our Ancestors: Kahnawake Mohawk Politics and the Rise of Native Nationalism*. Toronto: Oxford University Press.

Alfred, Taiaiake. 2005. *Wasáse: Indigenous Pathways of Action and Freedom*. Peterborough, Ontario, Canada: Broadview Press.

Anderson, Jeffrey D. 2009. "Contradictions across Space-Time and Language Ideologies in Northern Arapaho Language Shift." In *Native American Language Ideologies: Beliefs, Practices, and Struggles in Indian Country*, edited by Paul V. Kroskrity and Margaret C. Field, 48–76. Tucson: University of Arizona Press.

Barber, Katrine. 2005. *Death of Celilo Falls*. Seattle: University of Washington Press.

Beavert, Virginia, and Sharon Hargus. 2009. *Ichishkíin Sɨ́nwit Yakama/Yakima Sahaptin Dictionary*. Toppenish, WA and Seattle: Heritage University and University of Washington Press.

Beavert, Virginia, and Bruce Rigsby. 1975. *Yakima Language Practical Dictionary*. Toppenish, WA: Consortium of Johnson O'Malley Committees, Region IV (State of Washington).

Begay, Manley A., Stephen Cornell, Miriam Jorgensen, and Nathan Pryor. 2007. "Rebuilding Native Nations: What Do Leaders Do?" In *Rebuilding Native Nations: Strategies for Governance and Development*, edited by Miriam Jorgensen, 275–295. Tucson: University of Arizona Press.

Bird, Gloria. 2005. "Toward a Decolonization of the Mind and Text: Leslie Marmon Silko's *Ceremony*." In *Reading Native American Women: Critical/Creative Representations*, edited by Ines Hernandez-Avila, 93–105. Lanham: AltaMira Press.

"Board authorizes Indian Club trip to San Diego next fall." *Wapato Independent*, May 8, 1991, 4.

Brave Heart, M. Y. 1999. "Gender differences in the historical trauma response among the Lakota." *Journal of Health and Social Policy* 10 (4): 1–21.

———. 2003. "The Historical Trauma Response among Natives and Its Relationship With Substance Abuse: A Lakota Illustration." *Journal of Psychoactive Drugs* 35 (1): 7–13.

Brave Heart, M. Y., and L. M. DeBruyn. 1998. "The American Indian Holocaust: Healing Historical Unresolved Grief." *American Indian and Alaska Native Mental Health Research* 8 (2): 56–78.

Castile, George Pierre. 2006. *Taking Charge: Native American Self-Determination and Federal Indian Policy, 1975–1993*. Tucson: University of Arizona Press.

Child, Brenda J. 1998. *Boarding School Seasons: American Indian Families 1900–1940*. Lincoln: University of Nebraska Press.

Consortium of Johnson O'Malley Committees of Region IV State of Washington. 1974. *The Way It Was*. Edited by Virginia Beavert. Toppenish, WA Consortium of Johnson O'Malley Committees, Region IV.

Cooper, Matt. 1999. "1999 Women of the Year: Two Women Honored for Local Cultural Efforts." *Yakima Herald-Republic*, July 9, 1999.

Cornell, Stephen. 2007. "Remaking the Tools of Governance: Colonial Legacies, Indigenous Solutions." In *Rebuilding Native Nations: Strategies for Governance and Development*, edited by Miriam Jorgensen, 57–77. Tucson: University of Arizona Press.

Cornell, Stephen, Miriam Jorgensen, Joseph P. Kalt, and Katherine Spilde Contreras. 2007. "Seizing the Future: Why Some Native Nations Do and Others Don't." In *Rebuilding Native Nations: Strategies for Governance and Development*, edited by Miriam Jorgensen, 296–320. Tucson: University of Arizona Press.

Davis, Jeffrey E. 2010. *Hand Talk: Sign Language among American Indian Nations*. Cambridge, MA: Cambridge University Press.

Duran, Eduardo. 2006. *Healing the Soul Wound: Counseling with American Indians and Other Native Peoples*. New York: Teachers College Press.

Duran, Eduardo, and Bonnie Duran. 1995. *Native American Postcolonial Psychology*. Albany: State University of New York Press.

Evans-Campbell, T. 2008. "Historical Trauma in American Indian/Native Alaska Communities: A Multilevel Framework for Exploring Impacts on Individuals, Families, and Communities." *Journal of Interpersonal Violence* 23 (3): 316–338. doi: 10.1177/0886260507312290 [pii] 23/3/316.

Ferolito, Phil. 2010. "Obama Names Patsy Whitefoot to Education Advisory Board: Yakama Will Influence Schools at a National Level." *Yakima Herald-Republic*, July 2, 2010, 1A.

Field, Margaret C., and Paul V. Kroskrity. 2009. "Introduction: Revealing Native American Language Ideologies." In *Native American Language Ideologies: Beliefs, Practices, and Struggles in Indian Country*, edited by Paul V. Kroskrity and Margaret C. Field, 3–28. Tucson: University of Arizona Press.

Garroutte, Eva Marie. 2003. *Real Indians: Identity and the Survival of Native America*. Berkeley: University of California Press.

Goeman, Mishuana, and Jennifer Nez Denetdale, eds. 2009. *Wicazo Sa Review* 24 (2).

Gone, Joseph P. 2009. "A Community-based Treatment for Native American Historical Trauma: Prospects for Evidence-based Practice." *Journal of Consulting and Clinical Psychology* 77 (4): 751–762. doi: 10.1037/a0015390.

Gould, Janice. 2005. "Telling Stories to the Seventh Generation: Resisting the Assimilationist Narrative of *Stiya*." In *Reading Native American Women: Critical/Creative Representations*, edited by Ines Hernandez-Avila, 9–20. Lanham: AltaMiraPress.

Grande, Sandy. 2004. *Red Pedagogy: Native American Social and Political Thought*. Lanham: Rowman & Littlefield Publishers, Inc.

Grey, Minnie. 2010. "From the Tundra to the Boardroom and Everywhere in Between: Politics and the Changing Roles of Inuit Women in the Arctic." In *Indigenous Women and Feminism: Politics, Activism, Culture*, edited by Cheryl Suzack, Shari M. Huhndorf, Jeanne Perreault, and Jean Barman, 21–28. Vancouver: University of British Columbia Press.

Hilden, Patricia Penn, and Leece M. Lee. 2010. "Indigenous Feminism: The Project." In *Indigenous Women and Feminism: Politics, Activism, Culture*, edited by Cheryl Suzack, Shari M. Huhndorf, Jeanne Perreault, and Jean Barman, 56–77. Vancouver: University of British Columbia Press.

Huhndorf, Shari M., and Cheryl Suzack. 2010. "Indigenous Feminism: Theorizing the Issues." In *Indigenous Women and Feminism: Politics, Activism, Culture*, edited by Cheryl Suzack, Shari M. Huhndorf, Jeanne Perreault, and Jean Barman, 1–17. Vancouver: University of British Columbia Press.

Hunn, Eugene S., and James Selam and Family. 1990. *Nch'i-Wána "The Big River": Mid-Columbia Indians and Their Land*. Seattle: University of Washington Press.

Jacob, Michelle M. 2012. "Making Sense of Genetics, Culture, and History: A Case Study of a Native Youth Education Program." In *Genetics and the Unsettled Past: The Collision between DNA, Race, and History*, edited by Keith Wailoo, Catherine Lee, and Alondra Nelson, 279–294. New Brunswick, NJ: Rutgers University Press.

Jacob, Michelle M. 2006. "When a Native 'Goes Researcher': Notes From the North American Indigenous Games." *American Behavioral Scientist* 50 (4): 450–461.

Jacob, Michelle M., and Wynona M. Peters. 2011. "The Proper Way to Advance the Indian: Race and Gender Hierarchies in Early Yakima Newspapers." *Wicazo Sa Review* 27 (1): 39–55.

Kirsch, Stuart. 2006. *Reverse Anthropology: Indigenous Analyses of Social and Environmental Relations in New Guinea*. Stanford, CA: Stanford University Press.

LaDuke, Winona. 2005a. "Introduction." In *Grassroots: A Field Guide to Feminist Activism*, edited by Jennifer Baumgardner and Amy Richards, xi–xv. New York: Farrar, Straus, and Giroux.

———. 2005b. *Recovering the Sacred*. Boston: South End Press.

LaDuke, Winona, and Sarah Alexander. n.d. *Food is Medicine*. Minneapolis: Honor the Earth.

Lomawaima, K. Tsianina. 1994. *They Called It Prairie Light: The Story of Chilocco Indian School*. Lincoln: University of Nebraska Press.

Maracle, Lee. 1996. *I Am Woman: A Native Perspective on Sociology and Feminism*. Vancouver, BC: Press Gang Publishers.

McCarty, Theresa L. 2011. *Ethnography and Language Policy*. New York: Routledge.

McGhee, G., G. R. Marland, and J. Atkinson. 2007. "Grounded theory research: literature reviewing and reflexivity." *Journal of Advanced Nursing* 60 (3): 334–342. doi: 10.1111/j.1365-2648.2007.04436.x. [pii] JAN4436.

Meek, Barbra A. 2009. "Language Ideology and Aboriginal Language Revitalization in the Yukon, Canada." In *Native American Language Ideologies: Beliefs, Practices, and Struggles in Indian Country*, edited by Paul V. Kroskrity and Margaret C. Field, 151–171. Tucson: University of Arizona Press.

———. 2010. *We Are Our Language*. Tucson: University of Arizona Press.

Mihesuah, Devon Abbott. 2000. "A Few Cautions at the Millennium on the Merging of Feminist Studies with American Indian Women's Studies." *Signs* 25 (4): 1247–1251.

———. 2003. *Indigenous American Women: Decolonization, Empowerment, Activism*. Lincoln: University of Nebraska Press.

Million, Dian. 2009. "Felt Theory: An Indigenous Feminist Approach to Affect and History." *Wicazo Sa Review* 24 (2): 53–76.

Morgensen, Scott Lauria. 2011. "Making Space for Indigenous Feminism. edited by Joyce Green. Native Americans and the Christian Right: The Gendered Politics of Unlikely Alliances. by Andrea Smith Native Men Remade: Gender and Nation in Contemporary Hawaii. by Ty P. Kāwika Tengan Mapping the Americas: The Transnational Politics of Contemporary Native Culture by Shari M. Huhndorf." *Signs* 36 (3): 766–776.

Nadeau, Denise, and Alannah Earl Young. 2008. "Restoring Sacred Connection with Native Women in the Inner City." In *Religion and Healing in Native America: Pathways for Renewal*, edited by Suzanne J. Crawford O'Brien, 115–134. Westport, CT: Praeger Publishers.

Nicholas, Sheilah E. 2011. "'How Are You Hopi if You Can't Speak It?': An Ethnographic Study of Language as Cultural Practice among Contemporary Hopi Youth." In *Ethnography and Language Policy*, edited by Teresa L. McCarty. New York: Routledge.

Parker, Lisa Ann. 1994. *Wapato Indian Club: Traditional Dances and Stories of the Yakama Indian Nation*. Wapato, WA: Wapato Indian Club.

Raibmon, Paige. 2005. *Authentic Indians: Episodes of Encounter from the Late-Nineteenth-Century Northwest Coast*. Durham, NC: Duke University Press.

Ramirez, Reyna. 2008. "Learning across Differences: Native and Ethnic Studies Feminisms." *American Quarterly* 60 (2): 303–307.

Rigdon, Sue. n.d. Lesson Plans: Indian Cultural Class. Private collection, Toppenish, WA.

Silver, Shirley, and Wick R. Miller. 1997. *American Indian Languages*. Tucson: University of Arizona Press.

Skutnabb-Kangas, Tove, and Robert Dunbar. 2010. *Indigenous Children's Education as Linguistic Genocide and a Crime Against Humanity? A Global View*. Kautokeino, Norway: Gáldu Cála–Resource Centre for the Rights of Indigenous Peoples.

Smith, Andrea. 2005a. *Conquest*. Boston: South End Press.

———. 2005b. "Native American Feminism, Sovereignty, and Social Change." *Feminist Studies* 31 (1): 116–132.

———. 2006. "Heteropatriarchy and the Three Pillars of White Supremacy." In *Color of Violence: The INCITE! Anthology*, edited by Incite! Women of Color Against Violence, 66–78. Cambridge, MA: South End Press.

———. 2010a. "Decolonization in Unexpected Places: Native Evangelicalism and the Rearticulation of Mission." *American Quarterly* 62 (3): 569–590.

———. 2010b. "Revolution Through Trial and Error." *International Feminist Journal of Politics* 12 (3/4): 486–492.

Smith, Andrea, and J. Kehaulani Kauanui, eds. *American Quarterly* 60 (2).

Smith, Linda Tuhiwai. 2001. *Decolonizing Methodologies: Research and Indigenous Peoples.* New York: Zed Books.

Smith, Norma. 2002. "Oral History and Grounded Theory Procedures as Research Methodology for Studies in Race, Gender and Class." *Race, Gender & Class* 9:121–138.

Suzack, Cheryl, Shari M. Huhndorf, Jeanne Perreault, and Jean Barman, eds. 2010. *Indigenous Women and Feminism: Politics, Activism, Culture,* Women and Indigenous Studies Series. Vancouver: University of British Columbia Press.

"The Past Is the Future." *The Olympian,* March 1, 1993, C3.

Tsosie, Rebecca. 2007. "Cultural Challenges to Biotechnology: Native American Genetic Resources and the Concept of Cultural Harm." *Journal of Law, Medicine & Ethics* 35 (3): 396–411.

———. 2010. "Native Women and Leadership: An Ethics of Culture and Relationship." In *Indigenous Women and Feminism: Politics, Activism, Culture,* edited by Cheryl Suzack, Shari M. Huhndorf, Jeanne Perreault, and Jean Barman, 29–42. Vancouver: University of British Columbia Press.

US Census Bureau. 2010. *Selected Social Characteristics in the United States 2010.* Accessed November 4, 2012. http://factfinder2.census.gov/faces/tableservices/jsf/pages/productview.xhtml?fpt=table.

———. 2012. *Selected Economic Characteristics Yakima County 2012.* Accessed November 4, 2012. http://factfinder2.census.gov/faces/tableservices/jsf/pages/productview.xhtml?pid=ACS_11_1YR_DP03&prodType=table.

Uebelacker, Morris L. 1984. *Time Ball: A Story of the Yakima People and the Land.* Yakima, WA: The Yakima Nation.

United States Department of Justice Office of Justice Programs. 2004. Bureau of Justice Statistics, A BJS Statistical Profile, 1992–2002, American Indians and Crime. Edited by Bureau of Justice Statistics. Accessed November 4, 2012. http://www.justice.gov/otj/pdf/american_indians_and_crime.pdf

Vizenor, Gerald. 2008. "Aesthetics of Survivance." In *Survivance: Narratives of Native Presence,* edited by Gerald Vizenor, 1–24. Lincoln: University of Nebraska Press.

Wapato Indian Club. 1994. *Wapato Indian Club: PAH TY-MUU THLA-MA "Messengers of the Healing Generation."* Wapato, WA: Wapato School District #207.

Washington State Indian Education Association. 2012. *Educator of the Year 2012.* Accessed November 17, 2012. http://www.toppenish.wednet.edu/documents/Rosemary%20Miller2012.pdf.

Wilmer, S. E. 2009. *Native American Performance and Representation.* Tucson: University of Arizona Press.

Wilson, Waziyatawin Angela, and Michael Yellow Bird. 2005. *For Indigenous Eyes Only: A Decolonization Handbook.* Santa Fe: School of American Research.

Yakama Nation. 2012. *Wild Horse (K'u-see) Project.* Yakama Nation Wildlife, Range & Vegetation Resources Management Program 2010. Accessed May 14, 2012. http://www.ynwildlife.org/wildhorseprogram.php.

Yakima Indian Nation Tribal Council. 1977. *The Land of the Yakimas.* Compiled by Robert E. Pace. Edited by Kamiakin Research Institute. Toppenish, WA: Yakima Indian Nation.

Index

About the Author

Michelle M. Jacob (Yakama) is an associate professor of ethnic studies and affiliated faculty in sociology at the University of San Diego, where she teaches courses in American Indian studies and comparative ethnic studies. She also serves as the director of the Center for Native Health & Culture at Heritage University on the Yakama Reservation. Her work has been published in several journals, including *American Indian Quarterly*, *Feminist Teacher*, *Wicazo Sa Review*, *Social Justice*, *Societies Without Borders*, *International Feminist Journal of Politics*, *American Behavioral Scientist*, and *Race, Gender & Class*, as well as interdisciplinary anthologies. She engages in scholarly and activist work that seeks to understand and work toward a holistic sense of health and well-being within indigenous communities. Her work has been funded by the Ford Foundation, American Sociological Association, National Institute of Mental Health, National Cancer Institute, National Institute on Aging, and University of San Diego Faculty Research Grants. *Yakama Rising* is her first book. She is currently working on her second book project, which analyzes the social, cultural, and political meanings of Saint Kateri Tekakwitha.